BEN FOGLE

LABRADOR

THE STORY OF
THE WORLD'S FAVOURITE DOG

WILLIAM
COLLINS

William Collins
An imprint of HarperCollins*Publishers*
1 London Bridge Street
London SE1 9GF

WilliamCollinsBooks.com

First published in the United Kingdom by William Collins in 2015

20 19 18 17 16 15

10 9 8 7 6 5

Typeset by Palimpsest Book Production Limited, Falkirk, Stirlingshire

Printed and bound in Great Britain by Clays Ltd, St Ives plc.

MIX
Paper from
responsible sources
FSC C007454

FSC™ is a non-profit international organisation established to promote
the responsible management of the world's forests. Products carrying the
FSC label are independently certified to assure consumers that they come
from forests that are managed to meet the social, economic and
ecological needs of present and future generations,
and other controlled sources.

Find out more about HarperCollins and the environment at
www.harpercollins.co.uk/green

To all the Labradors who have loved
and been loved.

CONTENTS

Labrador – noun \ˈla-brə-ˌdȯr-\ *any of a breed of medium-sized strongly built retrievers largely developed in England from stock originating in Newfoundland and having a short, dense, black, yellow or chocolate coat and a thick rounded tail – called also Lab.*

PROLOGUE

THE BEGINNING OF THE END

'Don't cry because it ended,
smile because it happened.'
Dr Seuss

I called Dad.

'What do *you* think?' he asked.

There was a pause. Not because I was thinking, but because I knew. I knew the answer but I couldn't bring myself to say it.

'Then we know the answer,' he replied.

I burst into uncontrollable tears.

The twenty-four hours following that phone call were some of the most painful of my life.

The knowing. The feeling of betrayal.

Inca, my beloved Inca.

We took Maggi and Inca to the beach one final time. I carried

Inca from the car to the shore so she could lie with her paws in the water. Here we were on a beach again, just as we had been on Taransay when her life was just beginning.

I watched as her ears flapped in the wind and she lifted her nose to smell the sea air. Then, her belly covered in sand and seawater, I carried her back to the car and we began that torturous journey back to London. I couldn't look anyone in the eye. In the rear-view mirror I could see Inca's snout on Maggi's back.

Dad was waiting when we arrived home. I lay on the floor and sobbed uncontrollably into Inca's fur.

'One more night.'

I carried her up to our bedroom, put her bed next to mine and lay there listening to her deep snoring. I didn't sleep. I felt sick with panic and in the morning my pillow was stained with tears.

At 6am I carried her downstairs and fed her, then picked her up and took her into the garden.

'Give Inca a big hug,' I said to Ludo, who threw his arms around her.

'Where's she going, Daddy?'

'Up into the sky,' I said, turning away to hide the tears falling down my cheeks.

I carried Inca to the car, taking Maggi with us, too, and drove 10 minutes up the road to my parents' house. I don't remember much about that journey except that I cried uncontrollably all the way.

'Thank you, Inca,' I sobbed as we drove through the empty streets of Notting Hill. 'Thank you for being my best friend. I owe everything to you.'

I carried her from the car into the house, burying my face into her fur, and laid her on the kitchen floor. Mum, Dad and my sister were all there.

Canine blood flows through the Fogle blood. Dogs are family.

I lay on the floor, hugging Inca while Dad injected her. Her breathing became heavy. I could feel her heart pounding and the warm blood beneath her skin. I breathed the familiar scent of her fur as I nuzzled into her thick coat. I have never sobbed like that in my life. It was a primal, uncontrollable, guttural sob as I felt her heart stop beating.

I lay there on the kitchen floor clutching my best friend, unable to move. Wishing, hoping it was a dream, I held her lifeless body.

Maggi came and sniffed Inca. I wanted her to sense that her friend had gone.

'Where's Inca?' asked Ludo, as I returned home with Maggi.

'She's gone up into the sky.'

'Hello, Inca,' he said, waving to the sky.

I had lost my best friend. It felt like losing a limb. My shadow was gone. A flame had been extinguished.

I had loved and been loved. Now I had lost and I was lost. I needed to find a way back. Thirteen years is a long time.

It's been quite a trip, Inca and me.

CHAPTER ONE

SALTY SEA DOGS

The tiny boat yawed and bucked in the mighty ocean. Huge Atlantic rollers crashed against the vertiginous cliffs as seagulls wheeled above. A lone lighthouse stood sentry, ready to warn shipping of the hazardous coastline.

My salt-encrusted hands gripped tightly to the oars as we, too, heaved into the surf. A rogue wave caught the front of the tiny boat, sending green water spilling in.

We were a pinprick on a tiny ocean.

I had come to Newfoundland and Labrador on the easternmost point of Canada – often described as Atlantic Canada. This is frontier country; a tough, rugged coastline where the people are as hardy as the geography. It holds a lot of similarities with its counterpart on the other side of the Atlantic Ocean, the Western Isles of Scotland. The flora and fauna reminded me of Scotland, only larger.

I was with local rower – Pete – on one of the original

fishing skiffs, a tiny two-man wooden boat that looked like it would be better suited to a pond than an angry ocean. These were the craft with which the fishermen had, in better times, caught the cod that were once so prolific in these waters.

Like a detective following a trail, I had come here in search of the Labrador. It seemed wrong, coming to a place that was also named after a different breed altogether, but all the evidence seemed to conclude that Newfoundland did play a role in the evolution of the Labrador Retriever.

Despite a lifetime of travels to Canada, this was my first visit to this part of the country. A Canadian father had ensured plenty of summers on the lakes of Ontario, where I spent my time canoeing, swimming and fishing. Of course, there was also a dog. A mutt called Bejo that had somehow been rescued from the streets of Marrakech, in Morocco, by a family friend and had been flown to the Canadian lakes.

I had long wanted an excuse to visit this remote corner of one of the least-populated countries on Earth, and now here it was . . .

My journey to Atlantic Canada began in the rather inauspicious surroundings of Dublin, in Ireland, from where I caught my transatlantic flight to St John's, which must surely be the shortest hop across the Atlantic Ocean. We had barely taken off when we were landing again, just four hours later.

St John's is a rugged working port. I'm sure it had once been a very beautiful harbour, but the heavy industry and the presence of dozens of offshore supply ships servicing the oil industry give it a gritty industrial feel. The supply ships tower above the small buildings of the city.

St John's is considered by many to be the 'big smoke', but even with the majority of the region's employment opportunities and, therefore, population, it has a small-town feel. Colourful, clapboard-style houses dot the streets as reminders of the city's heritage. This is pioneering country.

Labrador and Newfoundland are collectively one state. Bordering Quebec on the west and the rugged Atlantic to the east, it covers more than 29,000 kilometres of coastline. At nearly 150,000 square kilometres, it is the same size as Japan.

I had come here, not for the landscape, nor the people, but in search of a dog famed for its fierce loyalty and ferocious love of food. A dog intricately tied to British culture. A dog beloved of families across the world and championed by countless prime ministers and presidents. A dog both used to sell loo roll and owned by royalty: the humble Labrador Retriever.

The story of the Labrador is as intriguing as it is complex. It is estimated that there are between 300 and 400 different breeds of dog in the world – the exact numbers are disputed by various kennel clubs which have yet to recognise certain breeds that have been crossbred over time. Of course, all breeds began with some sort of crossbreeding, but how did the Labrador evolve?

Breeds of dogs are variously broken down by the English Kennel Club into Hound, Terrier, Gundog, Utility, Pastoral, Toy and Working. While many will class breeds according to what they were bred to do, you can also categorise them according to geography: Welsh Corgi, Yorkshire Terrier, Afghan Hound, Bernese Mountain Dog, the Maltese, Rhodesian Ridgeback, English Setter, Hungarian Vizla, German Shepherd,

Irish Setter, Spanish Water Dog, Manchester Terrier, Norfolk Terrier . . . The list of dogs with a geographical tie is long so I won't bore you, but you get the gist.

The heritage of the Labrador, however, is much more complex and confused. Indeed, dozens of books have been published over the years with conflicting stories about the history of the world's most popular breed.

While it is widely accepted that the Yorkshire Terrier, for example, was developed in the nineteenth century to catch rats in the clothing mills of the historic county in Northern England, and the Border Collie was a working dog cultivated to herd livestock in the borderlands between England and Scotland, the Labrador does not actually originate from Labrador, the bleak northerly mainland region of Canada. I, like many, had always assumed it was named after its geographical namesake in Northern Canada, but in fact the breed has its roots, by way of Europe, in the Atlantic island of Newfoundland where, in the late eighteenth century, fishermen relied on a working sea dog of similar appearance to retrieve fish. In researching this book and the history of this humble breed, I have ventured from Portugal to Labrador, Newfoundland, and then full circle back to Europe.

The origin of the Labrador is a slightly confusing issue, not least because 'Newfoundland and Labrador' is the umbrella name given to the vast easternmost province of Canada. The two distinct land masses that make up the province are separated by the Strait of Belle Isle, a hazardous, ice-choked, fog-wraithed, treacherously tidal channel approximately 125 kilometres long and ranging between a maximum width of 60 kilometres to 15 kilometres at its narrowest.

In all probability, the nineteenth-century Britons lumped the far-flung area and its associations together just as writers of that era indiscriminately use the words retriever and spaniel. But there are two distinct territories under one geographical title and – just to complicate things – two dog breeds associated with the province, each named after the wrong region. The short-coated Labrador is actually from Newfoundland; and the shaggy-coated Newfoundland emerged at about the same time in Labrador.

The early settlement of Labrador was tied to the sea by the Inuit and Innu people. It is widely assumed that the Vikings were the first Europeans to sight the land but it wasn't until the Portuguese explorer João Fernandes Lavrador mapped the coast that the region was settled. Today the region is sparsely populated, with around 27,000 residents, most of whom work the land for its iron ore.

So how did this popular family dog, with its lust for food and cuddles, come to live in such an inhospitable terrain and climate?

To further confuse the mystery, another 'geographical breed', the Nova Scotia Duck Tolling Retriever, comes from Nova Scotia, just south of Labrador and Newfoundland. All three dogs have distinctive webbed feet, a water-resistant undercoat and incredible swimming abilities – they evidently share some genetic stock. Most historians agree that the native inhabitants of Newfoundland, the Beothuks, did not have dogs. Nor did the pre-Inuit settlers, the Dorset Eskimos. Others insist there would have been Inuit, Innu and Mi'kmaq dogs left by the region's Aboriginal peoples, as well as descendants of the Norse dogs.

We must assume therefore that the Labrador descends from a mix of genes from the various dogs taken on board ship by fishermen from Spain, Portugal, France and England when they set sail to fish for cod in the waters off Newfoundland.

Dogs were needed to guard the camps, to hunt for game and to kill rats and mice. They were a useful bit of kit. Breeds traditionally taken on ships from the early sixteenth century onwards included mastiffs, bloodhounds, spaniels and terriers. It is probably fair to assume there would have been a number of cross-breeds. Residents of Newfoundland kept no records or census of the dogs on the island so there aren't many clues for breed enthusiasts to mull over. In a footnote in his *Variation of Animals and Plants under Domestication* (1868), Charles Darwin states that the Newfoundland dog is believed to have originated from a cross between an Esquimaux dog and a large, black St Hubert hound. Others point out that Inuit dogs thrive in cold weather, but not cold water.

It still seems amazing to me that some of the world's most prolific swimming dogs came from some of the world's coldest water. But then maybe that was the point. The people had to find an alternative to getting in the water themselves.

But the Labrador is a dog that loves to curl up on the sofa or sprawl on the bed. They are never happier than with their heads lolling out of the open window of a Land Rover speeding along a country lane. Newfoundland and Labrador? Surely this was the land of the hard-working pastoral collie – a dog happier outside and often without human contact. There seems to be a great contradiction in provenance and character.

Today it is very fashionable to mix breeds together; the

Labradoodle is a Labrador and Standard Poodle cross, the Puggle is a Pug and a Beagle, but what breeds might have mated to create the Labrador as we now know it?

Many canine historians believe their genetic make-up owes something in particular to the Spanish Black Pointer (the aptitudes of obedience to a master and of being hard-wired to follow a scent) and to the Basque or Portuguese Shepherd Dog, which is notable for a herding instinct and a close sense of territory. But it was from a very large gene pool that dogs were bred on an ad hoc basis and trained over 300 years to meet the specific needs of the fishermen. 'There were many ways in which they could be useful,' wrote Wilson Stephens, in an article entitled 'The Lost Years of the Labrador' in *The Field* in December 1989. 'The slippery decks of trawlers, heeling when the nets were being hauled overside on the cod banks of Newfoundland, sent many a hard-won fish sliding into, and often through, the scuppers. Retrieving out of water may have been the ships' dogs' first and basic role. Not retrieving fish only. A sailing ship's rigging included many small components also likely to be washed overboard – blocks, pins, lines, and so on; a fetcher-back was more than worth his keep. Who ever saw a better dog in water than a fit and confident Labrador? It is bred into them.'

The harsh, rugged isolation of Newfoundland and the specific traits required of the dogs allowed the ancestors of the Labrador to evolve into fine, shapely dogs. The terrain and climate required them to be sure-footed on land and broad-chested to swim strongly and surf the strong and choppy Atlantic waves. They needed to be sturdy enough to haul wood on land and drag fish nets ashore, yet small enough not to overpower a fisherman's two-man dory craft. The fishermen bred these dogs, presumably matching sires with exceptional traits to dams of a similar calibre. Or maybe it was more rudimentary, simply monitoring the accidental intermixing. Whatever the technique, it somehow produced the much-loved, distinctive, water-loving retriever of today.

Like their namesake, the people of Labrador bear a unique mix of cultural heritage, borne of their historical roots. Their accent and language is a mix of Scottish, Irish and a mid-Atlantic drawl. On first hearing I was sure they were from Southern Ireland. To be honest I couldn't make head nor tail of what my cab driver was saying on the journey from the airport to St John's, with his heavy Irish drawl spoken in a kind of pidgin twang. Indeed, there are more varieties of English spoken in Labrador than anywhere else in the world. No wonder I couldn't understand a word.

The Aboriginal population of what is now Newfoundland and Labrador can be divided into three ethnic groups – the Inuit (once called the Eskimos), the Innu and the Beothuk – but the current-day population owes more to its European roots, being largely the south-west of England. Fisherfolk from Dorset and Devon emigrated in the hope of making their fortunes with the cod banks, but it is more likely the small number of Highland Scots and the Southeastern Irish settlers who had the most profound effect on the culture and heritage of Newfoundland and Labrador's current-day population. They bear the ruddy cheeked, wind-weathered appearance of island folk. Having spent so much time in Canada as a child, I was struck by how un-North American this region was. It felt they had more in common with Europe than with their Canadian brothers.

The mix-up between the names and geographical roots of the Newfoundlands and Labradors occurred once the dogs were imported into England and the Americas. The dog more commonly associated with Labrador became the Newfoundland – the giant, shaggy, bear-like dog beloved of poets Lord Byron and Emily Dickinson and immortalised as Nana in *Peter Pan* – and the smaller, close-coated dog (also known as the St John's Water Dog, the St John's Dog, the Lesser Newfoundland or the Little Newfoundler) became known as 'the Labrador'.

The word *labrador* has dual Portuguese associations. For a start, the region of Labrador in Canada was named after the explorer João Fernandes Lavrador, who in 1499 and 1500 mapped the coastline, labelling the vast, scarcely imaginable area 'Labrador' on topographical charts that circulated during this period. *Labrador* or *lavradore* also means 'labourer' or 'workman' in both Portuguese and old Spanish.

The Portuguese predominated other European fishermen during the opening decades of the sixteenth century, and the men who subsequently undertook hazardous voyages to these inhospitable waters would have been gritty, rugged sea hands inured to working the sails around the clock and enduring cramped conditions. So the word was 'in the air' in any contemporary consideration of the nature of the venture. Both in terms of the region and of the prevailing sailing-cum-fishing nation which set an example of reliance on its sea dogs, the name 'Labrador' was wholly appropriate for a hard-working dog valued by generations of fishing crews trawling the chilly waters for bumper cod harvests.

It seems indisputable that there is a Portuguese connection, but the earliest references all seem to originate in Newfoundland. One of the earliest mentions comes from J. B. Jukes in his book *Excursions In and About Newfoundland*, written in 1842:

> *A thin, short-haired, black dog, belonging to George Harvey came off to us today. This animal was of a breed very different from what we understood by the term "Newfoundland Dog" in England. He had a thin tapering snout, a long thin tail and rather thin but powerful legs, with a lank body and hair short and smooth. These are the most abundant dogs of the country. They are by no means handsome, but are generally more intelligent and useful than the others. This one caught its own fish and sat on a projecting rock watching the water.*

Could this have been one of the early forms for the Labrador? The breed that has become one of the most popular in the world? Loyal, handsome and hungry?

Newfoundland is still a rugged, bleak land. It is hard to imagine the hardships of those early settlers. This is a place dominated by the weather. Trees grow crouched and bowed to the curvature of the prevailing winds. The ocean bites into the coastline, tearing away at the cliffs. It is a region of natural wealth; where once the fish was king, today minerals and fossil fuels are the main export. The offshore oil rigs provide employment to those who still eke out a living here.

In one of the small working fishing harbours, a number of boats were tied alongside the quay – the *Mystic Voyager*, the *Cape John Navigator*, the *June Gale* – all weathered by the cruel ocean. Their nets lay on the harbour side, ready to be repaired.

I have spent time with trawlermen in the North Sea. It was one of the most miserable experiences of my life. A week being tossed around a mighty ocean, like a rubber duck in a washing machine. Cramped and stuffy. Hot and humid. I can feel the nausea returning just thinking about it. The sleep deprivation. The smell. The blood. The oil. The rust. The diesel fumes. It's like groundhog day. Haul. Gut. Eat. Haul. Gut. Eat. Haul. I wouldn't go back out on one of those trawlers if you paid me. Here, 4,800 kilometres away, on the opposite side of the ocean, are the same ships. The same fishermen. The same hopes and dreams. The same wild, violent ocean.

The skipper of my trawler had been capsized alongside his father and brother when he was just 18. They clung to one another in the frozen, black waters. Rescue came, but in the process he lost hold of his father. He was lost to the ocean – one of the many fisherfolk to perish in the cruel sea.

This part of the world holds many parallels to the Western Isles of Scotland where I have spent so much of my life. Indeed, it was here, on a remote island, that my love of the ocean and Labradors began.

The American novelist Annie Proulx gives a measure of the bleak landscape in her bestselling novel *The Shipping News*, which is set in Newfoundland. One of her characters muses on the landscape:

This place, she thought, this rock, six thousand miles of coast blind-wrapped in fog. Sunkers under wrinkled water, boats threading tickles between ice-scabbed cliffs. Tundra and barrens, a land of stunted spruce men cut and drew away.

How many had come here, leaning on the rail as she leaned now. Staring at the rock in the sea. Vikings, the Basques, the French, English, Spanish, Portuguese. Drawn by the cod, from the days when massed fish slowed ships on the drift for the passage to the Spice Isles, expecting cities of gold. The lookout dreamed of roasted auk or sweet berries in cups of plaited grass, but saw crumpling waves, lights flickering along the ship rails. The only cities were of ice, bergs with cores of beryl, blue gems within white gems, that some said gave off an odor of almonds. She had caught the bitter scent as a child.

Shore parties returned to ship blood-crusted with insect bites. Wet, wet, the interior of the island, they said, bog and marsh, rivers and chains of ponds alive with metal-throated birds. The ships scraped on around the points. And the lookout saw shapes of caribou folding into fog.

Walking along the coastal paths of Newfoundland, the vegetation and trees had become a vivid red, orange and yellow. I wandered among the fishermen's pots and nets. Traditionally this is fishing country and the dozens of trawlers moored along the harbour were now wrapping up for the season, hunkering down for the winter. It wouldn't be long until the snow and ice arrived; freezing the harbour and isolating the tiny communities further. The locals I met on my travels in the region had told me of 'black dogs' that still roamed these beaches; wild and untamed, some believed these were the ancestors of the Labrador.

Beyond the city limits, the weak late autumn sunshine illuminated the cliff edge on the most easterly tip of North America

– Cape Spear in Newfoundland. Huge rolling waves crashed against the rocky foreshore below as flocks of gulls feasted on a passing shoal of fish. The next stop due east of here was to be Cabo da Roca, in Portugal, the most westerly point of mainland Europe, on which I had stood many times and wondered what its North American opposite looked like. Now I knew.

The mighty lighthouse is a reminder of the treacherous nature of the ocean that has cost many ships and their crews their lives. This is a hard, tough land. Newfoundland itself is a huge island, almost twice the size of Great Britain, and for many months of the year the island is buried under 3 metres of snow, but during the summer months, the islanders have a brief respite from the cold. Although even in the summer months, Atlantic Canada is reminded of its Arctic geography, as swarms of icebergs descend on the island. Locals make good use of these icebergs, though, by making iceberg water, iceberg beer and iceberg vodka. They even collect washed-up shards which they then use in their gin and tonics.

Perhaps the most astonishing industry, here, is that of the iceberg 'movers', those individuals tasked with either blowing up or tugging away mighty icebergs that are blocking harbours or are in danger of damaging property. There is even a website called Iceberg Finder where 'iceberg ambassadors' track the movement of these mighty bergs, which are more than 10,000 years old and can weigh in excess of 10 million tonnes. Icebergs also bring polar bears – which use them as ocean rafts, sometimes depositing the fearsome predators close to human habitations – which has given rise to another local expert, the polar bear 'relocator'. Today, though, there are no signs of icebergs, polar bears or the sperm whales that migrate through these waters, just a vast grey ocean.

In another strange twist in the tail and connection to yet another country, the Labrador – now the most popular pet dog in the United Kingdom, the United States, Canada, Israel and Australia – ultimately owes its status to John Cabot, the famous Italian navigator and explorer whose name is honoured in streets, towers, academies, universities and golf courses around the world. Cabot's 'discovery' of parts of North America under the commission of Henry VII in 1497 is believed to have been the first European encounter with the shores of North America since the Norse Vikings landed in around 1000 BC. Some historians think that either Nova Scotia or Maine was the location of his landfall, but the official position of the Canadian and British governments is that Giovanni Caboto – to give him his proper Italian name – landed at Cape Bonavista, a rugged headland on the east coast of Newfoundland. He found a Utopian land of plenty and his discovery heralded an era of heavy European fishing traffic which, in turn, brought about the development of the versatile sea dog we know today as the Labrador.

On 24 June 1497, Cabot set sail from the port of Bristol, then the second most important seaport in the country. About 3,500 kilometres later, his ships gingerly negotiated the rugged sea stacks and steep cliffs of a *terra nova* to touch land at Cape Bonavista. By all accounts, he made a quick turnaround, excited to share the news back in England that his expedition had indeed found, discovered and investigated something unknown to all Christian folk – an incredible wealth of fish stocks off these shores. His crew reported 'the sea there is full of fish that can be taken not only with nets but with fishing-baskets'.

Today the cod or 'baclau' is still the regional dish. Fish and brewis, which is pronounced 'brews' is the most popular. The meal consists of cod and *hard bread* or hard tack. With the abundance of cod it became synonymous with many Newfoundland households as a delicacy to be served as a main meal. The recipe may vary, but the primary ingredients are always the same. Typically baclau uses salt fish which is soaked in water overnight to reduce the salt content, and hard bread which is also soaked in water overnight. The next day, the fish and bread are boiled separately until tender, and then both are served together.

The traditional meal is served with scrunchions, which is salted pork fat that has been cut into small pieces and fried. Both the rendered fat and the liquid fat are then drizzled over the fish and brewis. It tastes like . . . fish. Very, very salty, chewy fish. I had eaten the same on the island of Taransay when I was marooned there for a year. It was the only fish we ever caught. We were hopeless. We were living on what the local fishermen described as a fish roundabout. But we had no boat; no nets and no rods. All we had was a crate of salted fish. To be honest, I hated it and I still do. It makes me retch. The last time I had it was in the deserts of Oman; we took it in homage to the old explorer Wilfred Thesiger, who took salted shark meat. It was foul, but I ate it nonetheless.

I made my way through a hearty bowl of baclau as I sat looking out over a tiny harbour. A colourful, wooden-stilted fisherman's hut stood out against the gunmetal waters, the hard granite cliffs towering behind it. It was at once utterly beautiful and hauntingly severe. The view certainly helped the digestion.

The abundance of cod would be a turning point for the region and the emergence of the Labrador. Word spread quickly about the new-found lands and their bounty, and by the early sixteenth century, fishermen from Europe were regularly setting sail in a north-westerly direction and converging in the harsh and squally North Atlantic waters to fish for cod. The French, Spanish and Portuguese fishermen tended to fish on the Grand Banks of Newfoundland and other banks out to sea, where fish were always available. They carried an abundant store of salt and processed their fish on board ship, laying it down in layers strewn with salt to cure the fish. They did not attempt to dry it until they returned to their home ports. Without access to an indigenous source of salt, the English fishermen – travelling in fleets of vessels from West Country ports in Devon, Dorset, Somerset and Cornwall – sailed each spring and brought home a harvest in autumn. To eke out their meagre salt supplies and preserve their hauls, they developed a custom of salting the fish with a light paste, washing and drying it on long wooden racks onshore. This process required fish-curing stations to be set up on land. This meant they concentrated on fishing inshore (where the cod were only to be found at certain times of the year, during their migrations) and used small boats to return to the Newfoundland shore every day. In their chosen seasonal locations, English fishing captains at the turn of the seventeenth century reported cod shoals 'so thick by the shore that we hardly have been able to row a boat through them'. Some even talk of walking across them – during my short stint as an offshore fisherman I once saw a net of cod pulled from the North Sea, so full of fish that the trawler men could walk between the two trawlers on the fish.

Once dried, the fish were then loaded on board the ships and sent back home. A winter crew was left behind each year to stake out the shore, maintain the curing facility and protect the fragile and lucrative toehold that England had established in the cod-fishing industry. Permanent settlements were discouraged, so it is easy to imagine how those left behind would have relied on their dogs not only to hunt for food and guard their base, but also for companionship.

The cod moratorium of 1992 nearly devastated the region. The Canadian government declared a halt on the northern cod fishery, which for nearly 500 years had shaped the lives and communities of Atlantic Canada. The biomass of cod had fallen to just 1 per cent of its early levels and was in danger of complete extinction. Better fishing technology and trawlers had decimated stocks. It was a brave and bold decision by the Canadian government, and one that caused untold misery and hardship for the local people. More than 35,000 fisherfolk from 400 communities were left unemployed overnight.

Some communities never recovered. The effects of the moratorium are still obvious; there is an air of sadness that clings to the region like an Atlantic fog. A large imposing museum that soars into St John's skyline like an ugly carbuncle is symbolic – like a giant fish factory, there for all to remember. The museum is crammed full of fishing gear and boats. Photographs of weathered faces hauling, processing and salting cod. Huge piles of fish.

Nostalgic photos of a bygone era when the cod was king and the community thrived.

By the 1620s, tiny, isolated settlements on the coast of Newfoundland became home to fishermen and their ship dogs – mainly from England, but also from Portugal, Spain, France and the Basque Country – as competition over the best waters hotted up and everyone was eager to stake their claim on the fishing rights.

The first sightings in Britain of the 'St John's Dogs or Little Newfoundler Dogs' were in the late eighteenth century. They had been brought back across the Atlantic aboard the ships carrying their precious cargoes of dried and salted fish.

In 1785, Robert Burns's poem, *The Twa Dogs*, refers to a creature, 'His hair, his size, his mouth, his lugs/Shew'd he was nane o'Scotland's dogs/But whelped some place far abroad,/ Where sailors gang to fish for cod.' Could this have been the loyal Labrador?

In 1814, Colonel Peter Hawker, a well-known sportsman, watched Labradors at work on the trawlers in Newfoundland, describing them as the St John's breed of Newfoundland. In the first published account of a Labrador, his diary describes the dog as 'by far the best for any kind of shooting. He is generally black and no bigger than a Pointer, very fine in legs, with short, smooth hair and does not carry his tail so much curled as the other [meaning the Newfoundland, which had a rough coat and a tail that curved over its back]; is extremely quick and active in running, swimming and fighting . . . The St John's breed of these dogs is chiefly used on their native coast by fishermen. Their sense of smelling is scarcely to be credited. Their discrimination of scent . . . appears almost impossible . . . For finding wounded game of every description, there is not his equal in the canine race; and he is sine qua non in the general pursuit of waterfowl.'

Eight years later, in 1822, the Scottish-Canadian explorer William Epps Cormack, who was born in St John's, crossed Newfoundland by foot. He was the first European to journey across the interior of the island and it was during this expedition that he noted small water dogs, writing in his journal: '[they are] admirably trained as retrievers in fowling, and are otherwise useful. The smooth or short-haired dog is preferred because in frosty weather the long haired kind becomes encumbered with ice on coming out of the water.'

The earliest known depiction of the St John's water dog – owned by a Mr Alsop – was on the canvas of the famous animal painter Edwin Landseer in 1822. Initially entitled *Watchful Sentinel* and known now as *Cora. A Labrador Dog,* the commissioned portrait of a much-loved pet shows a black dog with white paws and chest lying inside a stable yard or carriage house, with horses and grooms working in the background and, interestingly, no water in sight. (The earliest portrait of a yellow dog is believed to be in the Bowes Museum at Barnard Castle in County Durham – a portrait in oils of Mrs Josephine Bowes painted in the late 1840s with a yellow dog called Bernardine at her side.) This seems to be the moment these early 'Labradors' made the transition from sea to land. These dogs, seen and admired for their eye-catching skills in West Country ports and harbours, were being purchased for use on land.

For a land famous for two world-class dogs, there was a

distinct lack of canine activity as I wandered the tiny fishing ports. I spotted a single working Collie. In the absence of either of the region's namesakes, I arranged to meet two of the region's living mascots. Gus the Labrador and Felix the Newfie are both employed by the State to greet people arriving in the remote territory, predominantly by cruise ship.

We arranged to meet in a tiny harbour that is now home to an artisan collective where artists produce paintings and knitwear. It was a picture-postcard, perfect location. Bright yellow fishing houses with faded red piers were reflected perfectly in the calm waters. Here, away from the rough Atlantic surf, I could image Labradors plying these waters collecting fallen fish and fishing tackle.

As instincts required, Gus belly dived into the clear waters. It was like an echo of an earlier time as I imagined his early cousins swimming in these very waters for the fisherfolk.

The extraordinary twist in this furry tail is that Gus's provenance owed more to England than it did to those early pioneers. Indeed, his distant relatives had come up from Portugal to this remote land, only to traverse the Atlantic Ocean once again, back to Europe.

For the fortune-hunting fishermen, dog trading had become a lucrative subsidiary. The sale of fish was the main business, but canny sailors also sold the ice used to preserve their catch and, increasingly, established a dog import trade. The dogs' water skills were much talked about. They feature in old stories as near-mythical water dogs, as fetchers of sailors' hats in icy waters and blustery gales, big-hearted, eminently trainable and intelligent. They could swim with ropes in their mouths and sometimes – so the stories went – paddled out to the aid of ships in distress. They retrieved whatever their master bade them. The proud seamen put on a remarkable show of human–dog teamwork for the quayside crowds.

Wilson Stephens wrote in *The Field*, 'No wonder that the deck dogs on the ships off-loading in Poole Harbour caught the eye of passers-by. Perhaps the crew men entertained the locals by throwing overboard things which the dogs would retrieve, demonstrating their expertise at diving in and swimming back with a load. Perhaps bets were struck. No wonder, either, that the impression they made caught the eye of the local gentry – strolling, as all men do, on the quaysides . . .'

One spectator was the second Earl of Malmesbury, an MP and sportsman, born in 1778. He kept detailed records of the game he shot and of local and national weather. A large part of his estate at Hurn, in Dorset, included the floodplain between the River Stour and River Avon, north-east of Bournemouth. Hurn is listed in the Domesday Book as 'Herne'; the name comes from the old English '*hyrne*', meaning a disused part of a field or the land created by an oxbow lake. The Earl was fascinated by these amazing water retrievers. Until drainage operations in the mid-twentieth century, the River Stour had been habitually liable to winter overflow, spilling over its banks so that water spread over the countryside, creating large watery meadows a metre or more deep. The land was crisscrossed with carrier channels to control the annual floodwater; for half the year it was, as one observer put it, 'a minor Venice'. The quantity of water was such that a raised causeway had been built around a 16-hectare floodable meadow so that the ladies of the house could continue to enjoy their carriage drives before stopping for afternoon tea.

I know the River Stour well. I spent much of my childhood navigating, rowing, paddling and swimming in its meandering waters. My school was built on its floodplains. A distinctive memory was of flooded sports fields; the river often burst its banks, creating a watery world. How many times I found myself wading through this very water.

So could this have been the very same river that helped give rise to the most popular dog on Earth? Was the answer there all along?

The early nineteenth century was the golden age of wild-fowling, and the sporting pride and glory of the Malmesbury Estate was the duck. With such expanses of swampy waterlands there were always plenty of ducks – but many a shot duck would fall where only a swimming dog could retrieve them. The Earl of Malmesbury and a neighbour, Major C. J. Radclyffe, who lived close to the watery hinterland around Poole Harbour, saw these Labrador dogs as the answer to their sporting problem. There is mention of 'the Earl of Malmesbury at Heron Court' using his St John's dog for shooting sports as early as 1809.

And here lie the crucial links between Poole in Dorset and Newfoundland . . .

The Newfoundland fishing fleet docked regularly at Poole Harbour, with its catch of cod and other fish kept on ice in the hold. After the fish had been sold, the ice was sought by local squires for their ice houses (typically a brick-lined hole in the ground, covered with a domed roof, and used to store ice in the years before the invention of the refrigerator). The Hurn

Estate had two such ice houses that needed regular re-stocking with blocks of ice. According to the late sixth Earl of Malmesbury, 'It was usual for each ship to carry at least one dog on board. My great-great-grandfather on occasions rode over to Poole Harbour, and saw these dogs playing in the sea and retrieving the fish that had not "kept", so had been thrown out. He thought to himself that these water dogs, who retrieved so naturally in the water, were exactly what he required for his wildfowling. In 1823 he acquired two couples and built kennels on high ground for them, near a bend of the River Stour, known as Blackwater, which was only a quarter of a mile above the official tide end of the river, and bred from these dogs.'

The genesis of the breed began as a private whim. The dogs so impressed the Earl with their skill and ability that he devoted his entire kennel to developing, stabilising and pioneering the breed in Great Britain. He was the most influential person in keeping the Labrador breed alive and kept his kennel well stocked until his death in 1841.

Poole? It seemed such an incongruous place for this pivotal moment in the adaptation and creation of the Labrador. Poole, the home of millionaires, Harry Redknapp and the RNLI. Poole, where not only had I spent much of my childhood but also the last two years filming an ITV series about the history of the place and its people. In all that time I had never heard any mention of Labradors.

The only way of finding out how this connection had come about was to leave Labrador and Newfoundland before the weather marooned me for the long winter, and head to Dorset. But before I left Newfoundland, I wandered down to the harbour side in St John's. There, in pride of place, are two life-sized statues overlooking the sea passage. The bronze statues stand proudly, their heads held aloft, a reminder of this region's most famous inhabitants, not some great explorer nor a political goliath but two humble dogs that left these shores. Today, there are now estimated to be nearly 30 million Labradors across the world.

CHAPTER TWO

FISHY TAILS

Despite her outdoor life, Inca hated the rain. In fact, the only thing she hated more than the rain was getting her paws muddy. She also detested anything uncomfortable under her paws: rocks, pebbles, pine cones, pine needles, mud, even puddles could sometimes stop her in her tracks. But rain was the worst for her. If it was raining outside and she was inside, she wasn't going anywhere. She hated getting her coat wet almost as much as her paws.

Like most Labradors, she lived for her stomach. Inca *loved* food. She loved food as much as she hated stepping on pine cones.

Rather contradictorily, although she hated rain and puddles, she loved swimming. Like a moth to a flame, she was often left completely unable to stop herself. She would sleepwalk, like a zombie, into the water.

I will never forget the first time I met the TV presenter Kate

Humble. We had been teamed up by the BBC as a 'TV couple' to present a new series, *Animal Park*, following life behind the scenes at Longleat Safari Park.

I had just returned from Nepal when I picked up a voice message from Kate suggesting I come to dinner at her house so that we get to know each other ahead of filming. Naturally, I arrived with Inca in tow. Kate opened the door, and before I had time to introduce myself, Inca had barged past, down the hall, through the kitchen and belly flopped into the large fish pond in the back garden.

She re-emerged above the water line with pond weed on her head. I half expected a goldfish in her mouth. What's more, she couldn't get out. I had to kneel and haul her out by the scruff of her neck, at which point she shook the stinky water all over Kate, her kitchen and me.

It gets worse . . . Inca then discovered Kate's beloved rats. Yes, Kate kept several pet rats. She's since got better taste and keeps dogs of her own, but back then she had rats and Inca loved them. She sat next to their cage, staring, drooling and singing.

Inca had the best singing voice of any dog I know. Some might describe it as a kind of whine, but a whine is like a whinge – it's a negative noise. Inca sang. It was a happy, positive noise. I liked to think she was serenading the rats, but the rats weren't so sure. They hid in the corner as this giant, dripping wet, black dog sang to them.

Kate eventually intervened, worrying that the canine song might lead to cardiac arrest on the rats' part. And so we ate dinner to the smell of wet dog. It was the beginning of a long friendship, though, so it wasn't all bad.

Another time I remember visiting the late Duchess of Norfolk at her home, Bakers, in Berkshire. I was dating her grand-daughter, Kinvara, and we had both been invited for Sunday lunch. As always, I arrived with Inca. It was a glorious summer day and once again Inca made a bee line for the water. In this instance, it wasn't a fish pond but an immaculately clean swim-ming pool. Before I could stop her, Inca was sailing through the air into the azure waters.

We weren't invited back.

Over the years I lost count of the number of times I hauled Inca from rivers, canals and even cattle troughs. And all this from a dog that didn't like to get her paws wet. It was all or nothing with Inca.

It is perhaps unsurprising, given its coastal place of origin, that the Labrador began its life as a Water Dog. 'It was as a water-dog that the Labrador came into Britain. Regarded as a water-dog only, except by the few who treasured them, and ignored by most, Labradors spent the next 50 years in the well-cushioned obscurity which is the privilege of specialists,' wrote Stephens.

It was in Dorset that the Labrador was first treasured and ignored in Britain. I have always loved Dorset. I even lived there for four years, in the army town of Blandford, which I remember used to be called 'An Interesting Georgian Town'. Perhaps it was because I spent some of my formative years there that I can feel my whole body relax when I arrive in the county. It has that unique ability to combine happy memories with a largely unchanged landscape.

Often described as Thomas Hardy country, Dorset is defined

by its rolling green farmland and its famous Jurassic coast. I have since returned many times both for work and pleasure. Indeed, I have spent the past few years based at Poole Harbour, making a series about one of the world's largest natural harbours.

Poole really is a place of contradictions, where hard-working fishermen moor their ships alongside Sunseeker super-yachts. There can be few places in the United Kingdom where there is such a jarring clash of the 'haves' and the 'have nots'.

Sandbanks peninsula is often described as the most expensive real estate in Great Britain, and even one of the most expensive in the world. Here, million-pound glass and steel structures look out onto the working waters where fishermen still ply their trades. That it was here that the Labrador was first discovered seems incredible.

The harbour wall has changed very little in the last century. Close your eyes and you can still imagine the hubbub of trawlers emptying their holds of cod after their long voyage across the Atlantic. This would once have been a bustling place. It must have been quite a spectacle.

Today, the small fishermen's harbour is largely ignored. A handful of small boats still work the harbour and the ocean beyond, but Poole is as much a location for pleasure craft as it is for working boats.

Next to the old harbour pilot office, overlooking the estuary and the Sunseeker factory beyond, is Poole Harbour's museum. The museum is full of old artefacts covering the harbour's rich history, where old, faded black-and-white photographs offer a small porthole into the bygone era. I asked the curator if he had ever heard about the harbour's connection with the Labrador.

Nobody in the museum knew anything. There were no records. No photographs. No documents or accounts. The only inference was the large section dedicated to Newfoundland and the Dorset families who emigrated in search of wealth.

I sifted through hundreds of old photographs hoping to find the famous performing 'black dogs' that had captivated Lord Malmesbury, but there was nothing.

It seems that Poole has long forgotten its part in the story of the evolution of the world's most popular breed. So while the connection between Poole and Newfoundland is strong, Poole's role in the import of the Labrador as we know it today remains a bit of a mystery. Back in London, at the British Library, I read the first page of the leather-bound *Stud Book of the Duke of Buccleuch's Labrador*. The book names Ned (1882), sired by Lord Malmesbury's Sweep (1877) and dam Lord Malmesbury's Juno (1878), and describes him as 'of a different category to any of the other dogs' at the Duke's kennels. According to the book, Ned was followed by Avon (1885), hailed as even better than Ned – sired by Lord Malmesbury's Tramp, with Juno again the dam dog. The carefully kept stud book represented the start of an official record of the Labrador, but in retrospect, it is a rare and valuable document which highlights some of the events in the development of the breed. Another entry describes the time Buccleuch Avon is said to have sired 'liver-coloured' pups: in 1892, the record states that two 'liver colour' Labradors were born at the Buccleuch kennel. Labrador enthusiasts then began to demonstrate a desire to preserve and safeguard the 'new breed'. Records also show that in 1899 the first registered yellow Labrador was born at the kennel of Major Radclyffe and named

Ben of Hyde. Was this the first time the breed deviated from the traditional black?

The colour of the breed has long divided Labrador lovers. Many still believe that black is the true original colour and that yellow and brown are mere anomalies that caught on. Certainly as a dog to blend into the landscape during a shoot, black is undoubtedly the best colour, although yellows can blend in well in some wildfowling situations.

Throughout the second half of the nineteenth century Labradors were carefully bred but still remained 'rarities if not eccentricities' in the sporting and domestic scene. Traded exclusively among the landed gentry, they proved themselves the most versatile of working dogs: hardy, reliable, efficient, gentle, clean and undemanding. The same traits that define them today.

The Field once wrote, 'One of the countryside's riddles is how and why a race of dogs, so dominant for only 10 years short of a century, could also have been so dormant for so long, a clear case of unrecognised talent.'

There is a truism here. In 1886 – 75 years after their arrival on these shores – J.H. Walsh, in his *Dogs of the British Islands: Being a Series of Articles on the Points of their Various Breeds and the Treatment of the Diseases to which they are Subject*, described the Labrador or Lesser Newfoundland Dog as a mere accessory to a certain lifestyle: 'As his use in this country is almost entirely confined to retrieving game, he cannot be included among the non-sporting dogs.'

How did the Labrador go from being a specialist wildfowl retriever prized by a small elite circle in Britain to being the world's most popular domestic dog? The answer begins with another milestone in history: the wide-scale development of the breech-loading gun in the late nineteenth century. Up until then, shooting was by muzzle-loaded guns, *i.e.* a firearm into which the 'shot' and the propellant explosive powder are loaded from the muzzle of the gun (the forward, open end of the gun's barrel). To go shooting usually meant several guns (people with guns) walking through a woodland, copse, moor, waterland or field, shooting the birds their dogs put up. This style of 'walked up' shooting (sometimes called 'shooting over dogs') remained customary until the introduction of the much more efficient double-barrelled, quick-loading shotgun.

Thanks to the revolutionary refinement in precision engineering and machining in the nineteenth century, breech loading – whereby a cartridge or shell is loaded into a chamber integral to the rear portion of a barrel – became the norm. It meant a significant reduction in reloading time and gave rise to the popularity of driven game shooting, where beaters are employed to walk through woods and over moors or fields (dependent on the quarry and the season) and drive game over a line of standing guns spaced about 50 metres apart. In driven shooting, the head count of shot game is much higher than in walked-up shooting, requiring pickers-up with dogs to make sure all shot or wounded game is collected. The advent of driven game shooting was the cue for the Labradors to come into their own. Only dogs could keep up with the guns.

But it didn't happen quickly. Wilson Stephens described the evolution in *The Field*: 'Although those to whom it had become second nature no doubt learned to reload them safely in half the time that we would take, the pouring in of powder, the ramming of the wad, the charging with shot and further ramming, all processes duplicated for each barrel, made driven game as we know it pointless. All shooting was over dogs, and those which quested or hunted up the game also retrieved it, as spaniels still do . . . With so little game on the ground at any time, and with no need to hurry because of the time taken to reload after every second shot, specialist retrievers were unnecessary . . . When the shooting scene changed with the development of breech loading, the Labrador was not only present in Britain, but was the only retriever available. Yet it was not widely adopted to meet the new situation. Instead, the flatcoated retriever became supreme. Perhaps the strictly functional, workworthy Labrador seemed plain beside the more elegant flatcoat. But beauty is in the eye of the beholder, and is not necessarily synonymous with usefulness. The flatcoat had, and still has, an unlosable handicap.'

Stephens continues to press their claims in comparing the retrieving processes of both dogs – the flatcoat's tendency to cast widely, downwind of a target, and then work slowly towards it, dependent on air scent versus the Labrador's 'direct line to the mark, followed by a tight-patterned working-out of a limited area around a fall'. Stephens notes, 'The extra distance covered by flatcoats not only takes longer but inevitably moves other game off the ground, to the detriment of the sport. When Labradors worked, more game remained . . .' He triumphantly concludes: 'Realisation of the average Labrador's superiority was sudden, positive, and has proved permanent.'

So when did the Labrador become popular away from the field? Perhaps unsurprisingly, the gundog was now known not just as the Labrador but as the Labrador Retriever, and it had become the gundog of choice for the British aristocracy.

The Victorian love of both dogs and pastimes led to the incredible popularity of field trials and dog shows. The first conformation dog show – a show to assess how well individual dogs conform to specific breed standards – was held in the town hall of Newcastle upon Tyne in June 1859. The only breeds scheduled were pointers and setters. The first organised field trial – a competitive event at which hunting dogs such as retrievers, pointers and flushing dogs compete against one another in a series of tasks – took place at Southill, in Bedfordshire, in 1865. Both sports gained a large and fashionable following.

In April 1873 the Kennel Club was founded to provide a set of rules and standards for the popular new pastimes. The very first sport recognised by the Kennel Club was the sport of Field Trials, which in this era particularly tested the skills of working gundogs and attracted large and appreciative audiences. In 1886, Charles Cruft, a general manager at a dog biscuit manufacturer, founded Crufts Dog Show. Billed as the 'First Great Terrier Show', it began with 57 classes and 600 entries. By 1891, the show was known as Crufts Greatest Dog Show. The venue was the Royal Agricultural Hall, Islington, and it was the first at which all breeds were invited to compete, with approximately 2,000 dogs and almost 2,500 entries.

As a young boy, I used to visit Crufts with my father, when it was still held in central London, at Earls Court, and it helped define my childhood. I loved going to Crufts – the noise, the smell, the dogs. My role in the show became tighter in 2006, though, when I was asked to present the BBC's live coverage of the show. I presented Crufts for two years. I can't say those years were as happy as my childhood recollections; the pressure of presenting a live prime-time TV show, and the interaction with a significantly haughty group of breeders who didn't like my style of presenting, inevitably led to a bumpy ride.

I co-presented the show with Inca, my black Lab, at my side. The show was dropped several years later, after the BBC ran a panorama exposé that revealed the slightly murky world of the Kennel Club and their breed requirements that often lead to long-term health complications for many breeds. In fact, Inca was a case in point. Her epilepsy was more than likely to have been caused by a limited gene pool. In short – incest.

I digress.

Back at the late turn of the last century, dog ownership was booming, and with it an appetite for specialised breeds that ordinary people could 'discover' as the dog that best suited them. Labradors had come to Britain as sea dogs. They were spotted and cultivated as wildfowling water dogs. As gundogs to the gentry, they acquired a fashionable social status attractive to the aspirational classes. Eager to please and eminently trainable, loyal and lovable, playful and energetic, the Labrador gradually became a great all-rounder, a symbol of social status, a valued working dog to some and a treasured family pet to millions. Once the development of breech loading revolutionised the shooting scene, the breed's gundog expertise was its passport to the millions.

I left Poole and headed to meet Lord Malmesbury's son on their old estate. The Malmesbury Estate itself was broken up and sold several decades ago, with the great house turned into apartments and flats. Driving through the gates and along the drive, however, you still get a sense of the estate it once was.

The River Stour meanders through the land, through fields that were once flooded from the heavy rain which had made the river burst its banks. The Stour had memories for me from my school days, just a short way upriver from where I was now.

My first port of call was the small keeper's cottage. Over tea and scones, the keeper explained to me how important Labradors still are for the shoots. We piled into a battered pickup and drove through the old estate to the remains of the kennels. They had long since fallen into disrepair, with just a couple of walls remaining, largely overgrown. Looking at what remained of them, it seemed incredible that the dogs that had once been kept in these kennels were more than likely to have been the progeny for the millions and millions of Labradors across the world.

It was about the same time that the Earl of Malmesbury was beginning his breeding programme in his kennel on the south coast of England that the fifth Duke of Buccleuch (1806–1884) and his brother, Lord John Scott, imported dogs for use as gundogs on the Queensberry estates, in the Scottish borders, from a Newfoundland fishing fleet which sailed into the River Clyde. They had also realised what an extraordinary dog the Labrador was and so established a kennel in around 1835. One of the Duke's dogs, Brandy, earned his name on his journey across the Atlantic. Having been sent overboard in a heavy sea to fetch the cap of one of the crew, the young dog spent two hours in the water before he could be picked up again, by which point he was so exhausted that the sailors had to revive him with brandy.

The brothers loved their dogs so much that when they went

on a yachting holiday to Naples in 1839, they took their favourite Labradors – Moss and Drake – with them: something that was unheard of back then.

According to records, in 1871, the Earl of Malmesbury's neighbour, Major Radclyffe – who had patrolled Poole Harbour with the Earl admiring the fishermen's sea dogs – imported a dog direct from Newfoundland. He was called Turk and would go on to sire the line that included Ben of Hyde, the first yellow Lab to be registered.

By the early 1880s the original Buccleuch strain had died out, just five or six decades on from the original purchases from the fishermen on the Clyde. This could well have signalled the end of the Scottish lineage of the Labrador Retriever, were it not for our friend the sixth Earl of Malmesbury who 'gave them a pair, descended from our own imported dogs'.

It is probably fair to say that a chance meeting between the third Earl of Malmesbury (at the age of 75) with the sixth Duke of Buccleuch (1831–1914) and the twelfth Duke of Home (1834–1918) saved the Labrador from extinction. The two Scots were visiting a sick aunt on the south coast of England and while there accepted an invitation to participate in a waterfowl shoot at Hurn. Precisely where I was heading now.

The Hurn Estate is another old estate that was broken up long ago, but what remains is managed by the current Earl's son, James Fitzharris. In an old pickup truck we drove through what was left of the estate that had once been the family seat to James's ancestors. Hurn Court is now apartments, and there was an air of sadness as we drove along the road that had once been the drive to the grand house.

It was hard to imagine what this place must have been like when it was still the thriving seat of the Malmesburys, in the family's heyday, when aristocracy had money and power.

'That's all that remains of the kennels,' pointed James from one of the misted windows of the pickup. There were some simple foundations and the skeletal remains of one of the walls. The remains had been largely consumed by the encroaching Dorset countryside.

It struck me that these sad, unloved, anonymous ruins were symbolic of our amnesia as to the provenance of the world's most popular breed. James explained that he still kept Labradors, but that his father, the current Earl of Malmesbury, 'couldn't stand them'.

It was lucky that the current Earl wasn't seated back in 1887 when the two Scottish visitors were impressed by Malmesbury's eager-to-please, efficient water dogs and recognised they were the same Little Newfoundler dogs as their father's. Malmesbury generously offered them some of his dogs to carry on the breeding programme north of the border, and the pair of dogs, Avon and Ned, that he entrusted them with are now considered to be the ancestors of all modern Labradors: the legendary progenitors.

And so it was that the Earls of Malmesbury and the Dukes of Buccleuch were instrumental in developing and establishing the modern Labrador breed.

In a letter written to the Duke, dated 1887, the Earl first used the name 'Labrador' in print. 'We always call mine Labrador dogs and I have kept the breed as pure as I could from the first I had,' he wrote. 'The real breed may be known by their having a close coat which turns water off like oil, and, about all, a tail like an otter.'

Inca had the fattest tail you have ever seen; it was more like an otter's tail – thick with coarse hair. It had never occurred to me that this was part of her heritage – the powerful motor and rudder to propel her through the water.

As I said, Inca loved water.

CHAPTER THREE

BANCHORY BOLO AND BEN

In 1999, I had been languishing in the offices of *Tatler* magazine in London and I was now looking for an escape. A way out. I wanted adventure. I was 24 and still living at home. I wanted an opportunity.

At that time the BBC were looking for people to be marooned on a deserted island in the Outer Hebrides for a year, beginning in January 2000. The project, *Castaway*, would later become one of the first reality shows to be broadcast in Britain. I applied and was chosen as one of 36 people to be shipwrecked on the Isle of Taransay for a year as part of a social experiment to see if we could create a fully self-sufficient community.

We reared our own livestock and grew our own crops. We built a slaughterhouse, a school and our living accommodation.

Each of us castaways had been asked to choose a luxury item that we could take with us. One couple had chosen a bed, another asked for a piano. Someone even opted for a home-brewing kit.

A dog. That was what I'd take. My own dog. A puppy.

Until that moment in my life I had led a relatively selfish existence. The previous 24 years had largely been about me. I had never had to think about anyone else but myself; the family pets were still the responsibility of my parents and I had never had to do an early morning walk with a hangover, or worry about a late night because the dogs were hungry.

This would be the moment that I made the sacrifice and took on a canine responsibility of my own.

But what breed?

I had grown up with Golden Retrievers; I liked Deer Hounds but they were too big; I liked Newfoundlands but they were too hairy; I liked Pugs but they had too many health problems. To be honest, I would have been happy with most breeds, but in reality there was only ever one breed of dog I ever really truly wanted: a Labrador.

Why a Labrador? Well, that is a complicated one, and it will take more than a chapter to explain.

Growing up above a veterinary clinic, I had more than my fair share of encounters with a wide variety of breeds. To be honest, growing up, I loved all dogs – irrelevant of breed, but I knew three Labradors in my childhood, two of which belonged to my late friend Alice Benkert. Alice lived in Esher, and the two dogs, Poppy and Oscar, would come with her parents to collect her from school. I would spend hours with them. I remember the time we came back to her home and the dogs had found several boxes of freezer bags that they had scattered like confetti around the kitchen.

The other Labrador belonged to an English teacher at my

school, called PJ. He had a beautiful black dog and a Land Rover – and I coveted both. Now I think about it, I wonder whether getting to know Labradors at the same time that I went to boarding school and was separated from my childhood Golden Retrievers was the seed of my obsession. I cried for a year when I left home. My homesickness was debilitating. It wasn't just that I missed my home, but also the dogs, Liberty and Lexington.

Lib and Lex, as we knew them, were my best friends and my confidants. They were what really made our house a home. They soothed and settled me. I decorated the walls around my bed at school with photographs of the dogs, but that only made things worse. I would sob into my pillow each night, wishing, longing for that warm, hairy body stretched out on my bed.

When my parents finally understood how much I missed the dogs, they decided it would be a good idea if they came along with us when it was time to drop me off at school. But the fleeting appearance of Lib and Lex only made matters worse – tears would stream down my cheeks as I watched my parents drive away, a small tuft of blond fur visible through the back window.

I'm getting homesick just thinking about it!

Lib and Lex were the first constants I really knew in my life. Both my parents would come and go, depending on work commitments, but the dogs were always there – tail wagging at the door, tongue lickingly happy to see me.

Throughout the term I would find their blond hairs stuck to my clothes. A reminder of my two friends waiting for me at home. Boarding school was the only time in my life when I was forcibly separated from dogs and it was then that I promised myself I would get my own dog at the first opportunity. Young naivety assured me this would be on the day that I left school, but then travel and girls got in the way and my plans got put on a back burner.

Until now. This was the perfect opportunity. The problem was that neither the production company nor the BBC wanted me to take a dog. To be honest, I never really understood why. I think it might have had something to do with the landowner who was leasing the island. While there weren't many ground-nesting birds on the island of Taransay, there was plenty of livestock.

The makers of the show argued that there were already three dogs, all Collies, coming along, and that a fourth dog would tip the balance. Not only would it be a drain on our limited resources, but it would also affect the fragile human-to-dog ratio.

I set about on a campaign to change their mind. I found as many cute pictures of Labrador puppies as I could and then got my father to draft a letter outlining the human benefits of having a puppy within the community.

We argued that a puppy would be a cohesive addition, helping to bond strangers and bringing peace and harmony to the newly created community. Bringing 36 men, women and children together in the extreme circumstances of a windswept, uninhabited Scottish island was bound to create tensions but, we argued, the presence of a young puppy could help to diffuse any emerging conflict and arguments. Maybe that's why they didn't want the puppy . . .

I promised that I would train the puppy to be a working dog

so that she would be an asset to the community. I was sure she could be trained to work with the sheep. And as for a drain on resources, I argued that she could quite reasonably live off scraps. She would be a Labrador, after all. They eat anything, I reasoned.

I'm not sure what clinched the deal for me, but the programme makers eventually relented and I set about finding my perfect puppy. A Labrador, of course.

Dad offered to help. For more than a week, we toured the country looking at litter after litter.

We drove as far north as the Scottish borders to look at puppies. Too thin, too fat – none was quite right. Eventually, detective work led us to a tiny kennel near Heathrow airport. There we saw a litter of black Labradors that stuck in my mind, in particular one of the puppies who was the last to be picked, probably because she was a rather scrawny-looking thing with a large swollen eye.

'Wasp sting,' the woman explained.

I examined her carefully.

'No thanks,' I said, rather heartlessly, handing her back.

As we pulled away from the yard, I caught a glimpse of her sad, dark eyes. Why was I turning my back on this lone pup? Suddenly I wasn't sure, but as with love, I wanted to be certain. How would I know she was the one?

For the next few days I couldn't stop thinking about her. It had been more than a week and I was certain she'd be gone.

'She's still here,' said the woman down the phone.

I raced back. We pulled up to the house and were led into the living room, where the puppy was alone. She had been weaned from her mother, which meant separating the dogs.

Immediately she ran up to me and licked my face. The swelling on her eye had subsided and, away from her greedy siblings, she was now much rounder, with a bulging pink belly.

She gazed up at me with her hazel eyes as I ran my fingers through her thick black hair. I nuzzled my nose behind her ear and inhaled her scent. It was instant love. I had always been told that I'd find her, and now I really had found 'the one'. I named her Inca.

I held her close as we walked out into the crisp winter night, but as we approached the car I heard a commotion in the background.

'Get back here!' cried a voice.

The puppy's mother had broken free and came bounding over. She jumped up and licked Inca clean across the face, then lifted her ear. I am not one to over-anthropomorphise our animals, but I swear she was wishing her luck. She was whispering something into that little dog's ear, and I'd like to think she was telling her to look after me.

As quickly as she had appeared, Inca's mother vanished back into the darkness. Her owner looked on in astonishment, a tear in her eye.

And so began a friendship that would change things forever. Little did I realise then how much this little dog would form, shape and create my life. She would change it in ways I never thought possible. The story of Inca is, ultimately, the story of me.

Inca and I became inseparable. I was still living in my childhood bedroom in my parents' house, and I can vividly remember setting up her little crate at the foot of my bed, feeling both fear and excitement at the journey that lay ahead.

My life of blissful selfishness was over and a new one of selflessness was beginning. I genuinely think that those two words separate dog owners from non-dog owners.

I guess, on the face of it, it is a little strange that we invite this hairy animal into our homes. We share our lives with a creature that was once undomesticated and wild. I've always been fascinated as to why we keep dogs. Why we love dogs. Why we mourn our dogs when they go. Of course, it varies from culture to culture and from country to country. Some argue it is a sign of development; the more developed a country the higher the number of pet dogs. The sharp spike in the number of pet dogs in China, with its emerging middle-class population, seems to back that up.

By the very late nineteenth century in Britain, the popularity of the Labrador was on the rise and it wasn't long before the Royals got in on the act, in a connection with the breed that has endured right up to the present day.

The first Labrador kennels were established at Sandringham by King Edward VII, then Prince of Wales, in 1879 to house a hundred dogs, and the Sandringham kennels and the Labradors that are bred there have become firm favourites of the Royal Family as a whole. In fact, it may come as a surprise to many that the Queen is as fond of her Labradors as she is of her infamous Corgis.

In many ways the Corgis are the public face of the Queen's canine companions, but the Labrador is the private love of her life. I was once told a story that the Queen has several Land Rovers custom-made with windscreen wipers on the inside. Apparently these were specifically adapted for her Labradors, who have a tendency to steam cars up from the inside out.

The Queen takes a very great interest in the Sandringham kennels. Since her accession to the throne in 1952, the breeding programme there has gone from strength to strength, culminating in the training of five Field Trial Champions. All the puppies born at Sandringham are named personally by the Queen and are registered at the Kennel Club with the prefix Sandringham.

At any one time, the kennels are home to about 20 dogs of all ages, including Labradors and Cocker Spaniels – ranging from the older and more experienced gundogs used by members of the Royal Family during the shooting season to the younger dogs under training as gundogs.

In addition to providing dogs for the Royal Family, the kennels also supply the Estate gamekeepers with working Labradors and Spaniels.

In a bout of hopeful optimism I sent a note to Her Majesty's equerry asking if it would be possible to visit the Queen's Labrador kennels at Sandringham. I was politely informed that the kennels are extremely private and that a visit would be impossible. While the Corgis are frequently photographed at the Queen's side, her Labradors are rarely seen and it appeared that was the way she wanted it to remain.

Records of the breed were kept by the Buccleuch estate in Scotland at around the same time that Edward VII was beginning his Labrador breeding programme, and it is these that note the arrival of two chocolate puppies or 'liver pups' in 1890. Could these have been the progenitors for the future of chocolate Labradors? The royal household would undoubtedly have given the liver pups the ultimate royal seal of approval.

But while the Labrador was finally establishing itself on our shores, across the Atlantic a problem was looming that threatened the strength and integrity of the breed in Britain. In 1885 the Newfoundland government, worried about the number of dogs in the region, passed the Sheep Protection Act which gave local government the right to impose a dog licensing tax as well as the right to prohibit dogs completely.

Inevitably, dog importations were affected. Colonel Peter Hawker wrote in the *Instructions to Young Sportsmen* that, 'Poole was, till of late years, known to be the best place to buy Newfoundland dogs; either just imported or broken in; until they became more scarce, owing (the sailors observe) to the strictness of those tax gatherers.'

The 1885 Act was meant to encourage sheep raising by reducing the number of potential predators, but the result was to kill the Labrador export trade. The Quarantine Act of 1895 created another barrier to the importing of dogs. The Act prohibited dogs from entering Great Britain without a licence and without first undergoing a strict six-month quarantine to prevent the introduction of rabies.

The future of the Labrador hung in the balance.

Between 1890 and 1930 the multiple taxes, restrictions and paperwork meant no new dogs were imported to Britain and the results were quickly felt. This was the moment when 'breed mixing' began. Some breeders began mixing Labradors with Setters and Pointers. 'Bearing in mind the high qualities attributed to pure Labradors, it is somewhat strange that the breed should have been allowed to degenerate by the various crosses of Setter and Spaniel blood,' wrote Hugh Dalziel in his 1897 publication,

British Dogs, Volume III, referring to new problems such as a hard mouth and sulky temper.

Within the tight circle of enthusiasts there was a move to preserve the purity of the breed. In 1903 the Labrador Retriever was recognised by the Kennel Club. In 1904, it was granted breed status and listed separately as a member of the Gundog Group. The breed standard was written, and it was almost identical to the one that holds sway today.

During the first decade of the twentieth century, Labrador Retrievers rose to prominence in the show ring and in field trials, and were also much favoured gundogs. By 1913, they were so well entrenched in the world of dog ownership that their qualities as working dogs were causing an emotive debate. The criticism that was voiced that they could be a 'bit hard in the mouth' was queried by Frank Townend Barton in his authoritative volume, *Gun Dogs.* The ideal retriever is a 'soft-mouthed' dog, a fetcher which picks up game softly but firmly to bring back birds that are fit for the table. Dogs that unnecessarily drop, crunch on, chew or even eat the bird before delivery to the handler are considered 'hard-mouthed'.

'If the Labrador possesses the qualities assigned to it by James Craw (at one time gamekeeper at Hirsel and Netherby), viz sagacity, stamina, perseverance, quickness and nose, then no other variety can come up to the Labradors,' he wrote. 'The only fault that he had to find with some of them – a fault common to all other varieties of retriever – was that they were a bit hard in the mouth. Gamekeepers and shooting men required a dog that could retrieve birds and game without piercing the skin with their teeth. I have always thought

Labradors have one of the softest of bites; indeed, I have even seen Labradors carry fresh, unboiled eggs in their mouths while running.

Controversy, however, has frequently arisen concerning this matter, but supporters often point out that this trait spans the retriever group as a whole. Sometimes hunger just takes over.

Townend Barton reasoned 'the Labrador was one of the best dogs in existence for a gamekeeper, most of which like their dogs to look 'well and fit' at the opening of the shooting season, without needing to devote much attention to them during the busy time, which necessarily precedes it on estates where hand-rearing of pheasants is carried on to any extent.'

Barton gives his 'strong recommendation of the breed to shooting men' on the eve of the First World War. The sixth Earl of Malmesbury recalls the estate keeper, Mr Beech, being called up into the Royal Artillery and '. . . the [Labrador] bitch he left behind pined so much that she sadly died. As a child I just remember her. She was the last of the direct descendants of the dogs imported in 1823.'

In the middle of the war, in 1916, the Labrador Retriever Club was founded by Lord Knutsford (then the Honourable Arthur Holland-Hibbert) and Lady Howe (then Mrs Quintin Dick), with a Mr T. W. Twyford of Staffordshire, to champion the breed, and Labs suddenly became the fashion. In 1916 the club authored the first Labrador Retriever standard. In the 1920s and 30s, King George VI and Queen Elizabeth promoted Labradors at shows through their kennel, and the King entered dogs in Crufts. In 1938, King George became Patron of the Labrador Retriever Club. In 1952, on the death of George VI,

Queen Elizabeth the Queen Mother continued as patron. Today, the Her Majesty the Queen is Patron of the Club and the Duke of Wellington is President.

The Hon Henry Holland-Hibbert, great grandson of the 3rd Viscount Knutsford, still has the stud book that traces the foundation of the famous Munden line of Labradors and, according to records, the original kennel is still intact on the Munden Estate.

It's strange how trails can lead you in circles. I had already traversed the Atlantic Ocean in an effort to understand more about the breed I love so much, and now I found myself navigating the North Circular around west London towards Munden House, a 30-room eighteenth-century mansion located in the suburbs of London, just off the M1. The seat of the Viscount Knutsfords since 1874, the estate is an oasis of rural calm in the embrace of one of the most urbanised parts of the United Kingdom. There is no great gatehouse, pomp or ceremony; a tiny gate leads the way through barley fields to the manor house.

Henry Holland-Hibbert moved into Munden in 1992, where his father, Michael Knutsford, is the current 6th Viscount Knutsford. Henry's wife, Kate Holland-Hibbert, met me at the top of the drive. She was wearing an earpiece because the house has become popular as a film, television and fashion shoot location and an army of film coordinators had temporarily taken over the grounds. Kate was keeping an ear on proceedings. She invited me into her warm kitchen where a black Labrador was stretched out next to the Aga. On the walls were paintings and portraits of various breeds of dog.

Both Henry and his father, Michael, then welcomed me warmly, as did the Labrador. Under strict Knutsford folklore, every Labrador belonging to the family must be given a name beginning with S. For the current Labs, the family had voted on Smudge and Scooby Doo.

There on the kitchen table was the stud book that I had come to see. Saucy, Sarah, Scottie, Sahib, Sober, Sceptre, Sermon, Sandfly . . . the list went on into the hundreds. It was an impressive list of 'S' names.

No one remembers why the tradition began, but the family dutifully continues it into the present day. What was more telling, though, was the straightforward approach that had been taken towards the estate's dogs in previous decades. Next to each entry was a comment box, and several struck me in particular: 'Picked up poison and died' read one entry; 'Distemper' read many more; 'Died, Swallowed a bone'. Others were a little more brutal. 'Well shot' and 'dead and not mourned for' read several entries – clearly a reference to dogs that were not popular.

The stud book records tell us that the first Lord Knutsford acquired a Labrador in 1884: Sybil, a bitch closely bred back to Netherby Boatswain. The book records a description of her being a 'wonderful good bitch, nose, pace, endurance and marking'. She was mated to a dog from Lord Malmesbury's kennel and thus the Munden line began. Munden Sixty, the result of a mating between Munden Sarah (a Sybil granddaughter) and the Duke of Buccleuch's Nith (a Malmesbury Tramp grandson), was born in 1897 and by all accounts was a much-loved dog. When he died ten years later, it was Lord

Knutsford himself who wrote those words in the stud book that had affected me so much: 'To the everlasting grief of all who knew him, this splendid dog died in August 1907'. Sixty was the sire of a bitch who was to become perhaps the most famous of all the early Labradors, for it was she, Munden Single, whose impact on the field trial world would change the pattern of working gundogs for all time.

Munden Single was born in 1899 to Munden Scottie, who had been bought from the Duke of Buccleuch's kennel. Her breeding was therefore almost pure Buccleuch and Malmesbury. Single was destined for a success in field trials and shows that all others have sought to follow. Single had already won prizes in the show ring, including a CC* at the KC Show, when, in 1904, she was entered in the IGL† field trial at Sherbourne. As the first Labrador ever to appear at a field trial, she attracted much interest. The newspapers of the day recorded:

> *Only those who were at the Meeting know how very nearly the Stake was carried off by the finest Labrador bitch ever seen on or off the bench. We refer to the Hon Mr Holland-Hibbert's blue blooded Munden Single – up to a certain point nothing could have stopped her winning the highest honours at the trial. One of the best shots in England, a man who has handled retrievers all his life, declared to us that Single was the best game-finder and the steadiest retriever he had ever seen.*

---

*The 'Challenge Certificate' is what the judge signs stating that in his or her opinion the dog is worthy of becoming a Champion.

†The International Gundog League.

Sadly, she didn't win because she mouthed a bird when bringing it to hand. Lord Knutsford wrote in his record book, 'she was too gross and I was to blame for not getting her finer. She was out of breath after a strong runner and resented its struggles'. Single had, however, done enough to ensure that Labradors were now well and truly on the map. She won a CoM (Certificate of Merit) at that trial, then went on to win others and continued to win well on the bench. When she died in 1909, her body was preserved and put on display, and it is believed still to be held in a museum vault. Lord Knutsford wrote: 'It is a bad representation'.

In the early days of owning Labradors, Lord Knutsford regularly showed his dogs and enjoyed some considerable success with them. In 1904 he won the first bitch CC ever awarded with Munden Single, and Munden Sentry won the only dog CC, awarded in 1905. In 1909 Munden Sooty won two CCs at Crufts and Darlington. In fact, during the first six years of ownership, when a total of 29 CCs was available, dogs owned by Lord Knutsford or bred from Munden dogs won 15 CCs.

In 1923 Munden Scarcity was mated to Dual Ch Banchory Bolo. There were six surviving puppies; Lord Knutsford kept two: Solo, a dog, and Singer, a bitch. Another bitch was given to His Majesty the King and a dog went to Lady Howe. Lady Howe's puppy turned out to be Ch Banchory Danilo, a dog described by Lord Knutsford as 'winning more championships than any dog ever known – or nearly so'. Munden Solo also did well at shows; at Crufts in 1927 he was entered in ten classes, won six, was second in two and third in another. The judge wrote of him, 'if there had been a little more of him in size, I think he would have been very near perfection.'

Michael explained to me that, alongside his great grandfather, it had been Mrs Quintin Dick, as she then was, who had been instrumental in the formation of the Labrador Retriever Club in 1916, becoming the first Secretary and Treasurer – offices she held until her death in 1961. She also became the Chairman in 1935 when Lord Knutsford died. She was in every way the driving force of the club and the champion of the breed in its formative years.

Lady Howe owned some of the most influential Labradors of all time: dual champions Banchory Bolo, Banchory Painter, Banchory Sunspeck and Bramshaw Bob; champions Ilderton Ben, Banchory Trueman, Banchory Danilo, Bolo's Trust, Ingleston Ben, Orchardton Donald and field trial champion Balmuto Jock, to name but a few. Lady Howe purchased many of the dogs she made famous, her keen eye quickly spotting the potential of any young dog.

Her undoubted favourite was Bolo, though, a dog that did so much for the breed. Born in 1915, sired by Scandal of Glyn (a FT Ch* Peter of Faskally son), Bolo was an eighth generation from Lord Malmesbury's Tramp (1878), through Munden Sixty and Sentry. His start in life was not a happy one and until Lady Howe took him on at the age of three, he showed no sign of the greatness that was within him.

Lady Howe worked tirelessly for the club, and by her example and encouragement the Labrador attained a position as the most popular retriever – which it still holds to this day. In the early days dogs were expected to be dual purpose and most of Lady Howe's dogs achieved success both in the field and on the bench.

* Field Trial Champion.

Served well by her trainer/handler Tom Gaunt, Lady Howe ensured that her dogs performed their task successfully at the highest levels. It is very significant that four of the ten dual champions in the breed were owned by Lady Howe.

Together, Lady Howe and Lord Knutsford were great protectors of the breed. He frequently went into print to defend the Labrador. There were constant disputes as to the breed's origins and Lord Knutsford was tireless in his endeavours to get to the true beginnings. There are notes of conversations with Major Radclyffe and Mr Stuart-Menzies, and letters to and from other early breeders. His kennel records describe dogs variously as being Newfoundland-type, Labrador-type, long- and rough-coated, smooth-coated, and frequently they had white markings.

Like so many other kennels, Munden had to endure a number of serious distemper outbreaks. Many promising puppies, and indeed some good adults, were lost. Lord Knutsford worked very hard to find a solution to the scourge. Having had little success in his approaches to the Ministry of Agriculture and the Royal Veterinary College, he finally persuaded the editor of *The Field* to set up an investigation into the disease. Funds were raised, the research was successful and a vaccine was eventually produced in 1929. *The Daily Telegraph* in that year reported that two vaccines were now available, albeit in very small supplies. The report went on: 'dog owners have every reason to be grateful to Mr Holland-Hibbert for the idea and to the great sporting newspaper for the manner in which it has been made possible.'

Michael is a charming man, oozing passion for Labradors. He has personally supplied many dogs to Her Majesty, and the

Queen has often lamented to him how much she wished she could spend more time with her beloved Labradors. Indeed, Michael told me the tale of one such of her dogs. The Queen had a particular soft spot for one Lab and decided to bring it to Windsor Castle so she could spend more time with it. She fed it and walked it herself, but the poor dog pined for its mates back at Sandringham and so she eventually sent it back for the sake of the dog. Even the Queen thinks of her dogs first.

It's another anecdote of the powerful emotional command that Labradors have over us all.

Smudge nuzzled my knee in an effort to gain my attention. Labradors do this; they try to lift your hand in an effort to encourage you to stroke them. Smudge had a litter of eight puppies. Michael recounted how horrified his wife had been to discover that only four were black. Of the two yellows, she exclaimed, 'what a shame', and of the two chocolates she lamented, 'how disappointing'. Colour is still an emotive subject amongst the purists. It seems that, despite the Queen's approval, many still agree with the old fashion adage, 'any colour as long as it's black'.

'Would you like to see the kennel?' asked Kate, as she led me outside.

Nat Parker, the actor, sidled past me, as a director in a clichéd leather jacket and aviator sunglasses barked orders to the hundreds of foot soldiers. They were in the midst of filming *Outcast*.

Next to the house was an anonymous empty kennel.

'There it is,' smiled Henry.

'It's not much to look at,' he explained. 'We don't use it any more.'

Like the Hurn Kennels, it was a forgotten, neglected part of the Labrador's history.

Before I left, Michael told me a little about his great-grandfather.

'The greatest anecdote about my great-grandfather, really, is from when he was speaking in his capacity as Chairman of the Labrador Retriever Club at the end of a field trial at Idsworth in 1935. He spoke, sat down with a drink in hand, collapsed and died. They carried him out in a box but everyone agreed it was the happiest way for him to go.'

Before leaving, I asked Henry about the provenance of their current Munden Labradors. He told me the story of a chance encounter.

'When we got our Lab, who's now 12 years old, my wife went to a breeder whose dogs she'd admired out walking. Knowing the family history, we explained that we were particularly keen to find a puppy that came from the Munden line. "That's easy," the breeder laughed. "Almost all Labradors are descended from the Munden line." We thought we'd be unearthing something really special, but it turns out the Munden dogs are not dissimilar to Adam and Eve for humans!'

The breeder's name was Sussie Wiles, someone I would later meet myself.

Across the Atlantic at the end of the nineteenth century, things were picking up for the Labrador, too, although it wasn't until the late 1920s that the American Kennel Club recognised the Labrador Retriever as a separate breed. The first registration of Labradors by the AKC was in 1917, and in the early 1920s an influx of British dogs had begun to form the backbone of the breed in the United States. Distinguished Long Island families began to compete them in dog shows and retrieving trials, but they were an elite presence. A 1928 *American Kennel Gazette* article, entitled 'Meet the Labrador Retriever', ushered in a wider recognition of its traits as both game finders and water dogs. Up until those words were written in the United States, the American Kennel Club had only registered 23 Labradors in the country.

By the 1930s the 'St John's dog' was rare in Newfoundland, and the 6th Duke of Buccleuch was only finally able to import a few more dogs between 1933 and 1934 to continue the line. The advent of the Second World War in 1939, with six tough years of food shortages and rationing, took its toll on breeding kennels. In many cases, dogs had to be fed on meat that was unfit for human consumption. Soon after the war, an epidemic of hardpad distemper killed significant numbers of dogs; a high proportion of the survivors were left with crippling chorea, a nasty disease of the nervous system also known as St Vitus's Dance. Nevertheless, a core number of top-quality Labradors remained. Over the next four decades, the number increased by 300 per cent. After the war, there was a marked increase in the popularity of yellow Labs, and in 1960, the first chocolate champion was hailed.

The temperament of Labs and their abilities were perfect for all sorts of roles as working dogs; so much so that by 1952, the dog formerly prized solely as a sea dog, then wildfowling retriever, then gundog, became the popular all-round dog of today and the ultimate family pet.

'The Labrador Retriever is without question the most popular retriever breed today, both for work and show,' wrote P. R. A.

Moxon in *Gundogs: Training & Field Trials.* 'A comparatively "new" breed, Labradors have won the esteem of shooting men by their outstanding ability to be trained, find game and become companions and guards. The Labrador, as a breed, can be said to be both fast and stylish in action, unequalled in water and with "trainability" far above that of other breeds, and a devotion to master or mistress that makes them ideal companions. The smooth, short coat has many advantages readily appreciated by the housewife and the car owner. Dogs from working strains almost train themselves to the gun.'

As Wilson Stephens concluded in his definitive paper on the lost years of the Labrador, 'Their versatility stems from a stolidity of temperament which makes them neither exciting nor excitable. It combines with an inherited eagerness to do what is expected of them. Their family tradition of jumping into a rough and icy sea whenever ordered to do so has now been transferred to many other functions outside sport.'

The wide-ranging usefulness of the Labrador sees them valued as guide dogs for the blind, by Customs officers for drug detection, by the police and the military for mine and explosive location, by rescue services, security guards and counterfeit detection experts as well as in a new field of medical detection. They carry out their duties with a sense of decorum. 'Labradors set a tone for the occasions they grace. Their presence means that serious business is going on. The hazardous, often grim, North Atlantic scene seems a strange origin for these omnipresent participants in typically British occasions,' wrote Stephens.

I love that sense of decorum that is prevalent in Labs. It isn't a nose-in-the-air kind of arrogance that some breeds exude, it is more humble. They hold up their heads with pride, assured of their loyalty and ability. Perhaps this is the reason why the Labrador Retriever has been declared the most popular breed in the United States for nearly 24 consecutive years. More than 60 years on, Labradors hold universal appeal which makes them the most popular breed of dog by registered ownership not just in the United States, but also in Australia, Canada, New Zealand, the United Kingdom and Israel.

CHAPTER FOUR

THE INCREDIBLE JOURNEY

Inca, Inca-pinka, Incala pinkala, Pink, Pinky, Stink, Stinkalot, Incapotamus, Stincapotamus, Inca bazinka, Ink, Inky. Like most dogs, Inca had many names.

I had thought about calling her Tatty when I first got her, but I eventually plumped for Inca, in part because I had known one other dog called Inca, a large black mongrel I had met while studying in Costa Rica. She had belonged to an English family that owned a macadamia nut farm in the rainforest.

Dog names are a funny business. Does the dog grow into its name or does the name affect the behaviour and temperament of the dog? Maybe we project a personality according to name. I've always found it comical to meet dogs with human names, like Gary, Charlie or Kevin. There is something comedic about it.

In my mind, she was only ever really an Inca. Having studied Latin American Studies at university and spent the best part of three years living in Central and South America, I liked the nod towards my own travelling heritage.

In fact, her pedigree name was Camilla, but she was NEVER a Camilla. Camilla was far too feminine for Inca. She was more of a tomboy; masculine in both her appearance and her personality. This was helped by her early obsession with humping anything and everything – there was a teddy bear that she would grab onto by one ear and hump for hours on end, or she would scrunch up towels and carpets and dry hump all day.

Despite her masculine build, Inca had the prettiest face. She had a thin stripe of fur down the centre of her nose where two directions of hair met like a wave. I liked to call it her honesty stripe. It really defined her face. If you don't have a dog, and you ever wonder how you can distinguish one dog from another, it's often these little features. I always recognised Inca by her honesty stripe – that and her enormous thighs.

She also had the biggest paws you have ever seen. They were like lion's feet. Huge. They weren't in proportion to the rest of her body. She had long tufts of fur that would stick between the pads. If you came across her paw prints on a beach or along a muddy trail, you would be convinced it was some kind of big cat.

As a puppy she was lean and trim. Her coat was glossy and black, but as the years marched on, both her body and her coat filled out. Just like her paws, her coat began to resemble a lion's mane. It was thick and wiry, so much so that people would often mistake her for another breed.

Inca was, and still remains, the funniest dog I ever knew. She could make me laugh just by looking at me. Maybe it was some of the nuances mentioned above, or just because I knew her so well, but she could make me smile with a flick of the eye or a bound of the legs.

Dogs have that effect on us. They get beneath our skin; we live, breathe and smell them. We are more like care-home nurses than owners. We are responsible 24/7. A dog relies on us for everything – food, walks, warmth, affection, company. We in turn begin to recognise every little quirk and foible. We recognise the smell of their farts and the colour of their poo. We can recognise their gait and bark from a long distance and we begin to see traits that would be invisible to anyone else.

It is with this familiarity that a deep, powerful flame of love begins to glow.

It is also the foundation for the anthropomorphism, the process whereby we give our dogs, or any animals for that matter, a voice. At first it starts as just baby talk, but as you get to know your dog, it progresses to an all-out personality, complete with voice.

I always imagined Inca would have a deep, rasping voice. It was probably a little unfair, but probably quite accurate. In my mind she sounded like a cross between Dame Edna and the Queen. When no one was around, I would find myself having full conversations with Inca and would give her answers in this slightly ludicrous voice. I would love to know what Inca thought of these bizarre, rambling conversations.

My father had suggested I get Inca a few months before we headed for the island in an effort to get her used to urban life before we headed into the wilderness, so that it would help her reintegration to the city at the end of the year. To do this I took her on buses, the Tube, into pubs and even to work. I was still working for *Tatler* magazine, so I took her into the office with

me each day. Suddenly I found myself more popular with the
girls. There were several office Pekingese dogs that belonged to
two of the writers and Inca joined them. I can remember Inca
falling asleep on my desk, hidden in a vast pile of paperwork.

Then, on Boxing Day morning, my parents drove us to
Victoria coach station, where Inca and I would embark on the
journey of a lifetime. I can remember waving as the bus pulled
away, my mother in tears. But I didn't feel so sad saying goodbye;
this time, as they turned away and left, I wasn't alone.

When we arrived on the island of Taransay, Inca and I largely
kept to ourselves – and later more so. Without Inca, I'm not
sure how well I would have fared for the whole year. She was
my reason – and excuse – to go off and explore the island;
indeed, we rechristened one of the hills Inca Ra because she and
I spent so much time there. Inca and I shared a cold little room
together in one of the eco pods in which we lived. A tiny, inef-
ficient woodburning stove was used to heat each room. The
problem was that it was only large enough to burn tiny twigs
in it. Ice would form on the inside of the windows. I built Inca
a little bed on stilts to keep her off the freezing ground.

Inca enchanted everyone she met on the *Castaway* island of
Taransay and soon she became an integral part of our community. Having her was not without its mishaps, though. Just a
week into the project, she had to be helicoptered off the island
to the local vet in Stornoway after cutting her foot open on a
shard of glass. Months later, she was caught in flagrante with a
visiting shepherd's dog and once again was helicoptered away
for the morning-after pill.

In the beginning she was allowed into the communal 'steading' in which we would all gather, but after a heated debate about dogs on the island, she was banned. Dogs had become a divisive issue on Taransay. For the first time in my life, I found myself living alongside people who disliked dogs. Having been surrounded with dogs all my life, it seemed incomprehensible that anyone could dislike the animals, but the numbers of this group had recently swelled dramatically due to an unforeseeable event . . .

One of the Collies, Fran, that had come along with her canine sister with Trish Prater and her two children, had, unbeknownst to Trish, arrived on the island pregnant, and nine weeks after we settled on the island, she gave birth to a litter of puppies. Not everyone was happy about this, particularly when two of the Castaways decided to keep puppies for themselves. Suddenly the number of permanent doggy inhabitants within the small community rose from four to six, which further irritated the dog dislikers amongst us.

I recall one particularly noisy and passionate community meeting in which the doctor and his family threatened to leave if all the dogs stayed. Not only were they concerned about a rise in the amount of dog shit around the island, but they were also concerned about the safety of their children.

Although I knew the dissatisfaction wasn't specifically directed at Inca and me, I felt guilty as a dog owner and the two of us began to retreat from social gatherings.

Another time we found a sheep that had been attacked. It was bloody and wounded. Apart from the odd stoat, the island had no predators and it was reasonable enough to assume that one of the dogs was responsible. But which one? I would have put my life on the line to guarantee it wasn't my passive Inca, but once again the eyes of suspicion fell on all of us.

Every time something happened involving any of the dogs, Inca and I would be summoned to a meeting to explain ourselves. It was slightly exhausting and, if I'm honest, I slightly resented those additional dogs. Inca had come with me as my luxury item, and only after a long campaign to justify what she would bring to the community, but the two new pups were like stowaways who had gatecrashed the party and added tension rather than diffused it.

During the year we had to keep video diaries to document what we were feeling or what had happened to us. One of the rooms in the little farmhouse on the island had been converted into the diary room. It consisted of a chair and a camera mounted on a tripod. One day I thought it would be funny if Inca left a diary message. I lifted her onto the chair and made sure her face was in shot, then I stood behind the camera and acted as her voice. I even waved some bread around to get her to move her head for emphasis! It was Inca's take on island life, and the viewers loved it.

Inca and I spent our year on the island hidden away in our icy little room, huddled under a blanket together, or walking together for hours on end. We knew that island better than most. We knew every boggy patch, each break in the fence and every loch. We walked and walked and walked. As summer approached, Inca would swim in the azure waters. Seals would pop up to see her. I often wondered if they thought she was one of them, or vice versa.

If I close my eyes I can smell the machair and the salty air. I can see Inca's black body bounding across the island, leaping like a spring lamb. It still makes me smile. Those were some of my happiest memories. Ever. Just me and Inca.

I would wrap up in my waterproofs and we would set off to one of our favourite spots. I had so many, but my absolute favourite was the north-west side of the island. There, we would settle into the soft grass. I'd lean against Inca's body and we would spend hours staring out to the ocean beyond.

I will never forget those views. Fear, happiness, frustration, hope and excitement all at the same time – that view presented such a conflict, such a contradiction. It was the watery moat that imprisoned me on that windswept island, but it was also the open ocean that led to exciting new opportunities.

I would stare at that horizon and imagine where my life was going to take us. My little black dog and I had a whole life ahead of us. The thought filled me with fear and excitement at the same time.

Inca's lifelong obsession with food began on that island. Labradors love food but Inca *loved* food. In fact, it didn't even have to be food, it just had to be consumable – and even that was open to negotiation. Sheep poo and seaweed were always a sure bet, but it was the discovery of the compost heap that had the most impact. Inca disappeared one day, only to reappear an hour later looking like a barrel. Or rather, she didn't so much look like a barrel as look like she'd swallowed a barrel. All of her features were in proportion except for this hideously distended stomach, at the end of which was her tail, wagging furiously.

I couldn't work out where she had found so much to eat, and then the next day it happened again – and then again. I began seriously to worry and even contemplated asking the production team if they could send a muzzle over. I worried that she was eating herself to death. The source of all this food remained a mystery until one day I found her chewing on an old tea bag. I followed the tea-leaf trail to the enormous compost pile where we would throw all of our leftovers, which was a not inconsiderable amount of food, considering there were 36 of us.

But soon the compost heap became a distant memory for Inca, as a thoughtful gift from a stranger became all consuming – and consumed. Unbeknownst to us, both Inca and I had been getting rather a lot of media coverage back on the mainland. The first we knew of it was when the monthly mailbag arrived, brimming with letters from complete strangers, addressed to me and Inca. In fact, there were some deliveries in which Inca received more fan mail than me. She was sent bones and chews and little knitted booties to protect her feet, and even dozens of photographs of other dogs sent by their owners.

One of these parcels contained a dog toy in the form of a squeaky lemon. It was nicknamed Mr Lemon and Inca loved it. Mr Lemon went everywhere with her. If I ever spotted the yellow toy lying around, I could be sure that Inca wasn't far.

I didn't need to worry, though, because Inca never went far. Until one Saturday, when she disappeared. I searched in all the usual places – the kitchen, the storage shed, the compost heap the abattoir. I looked everywhere. No Inca.

I didn't panic at first. An hour passed and there was still no sign. None of the other castaways had seen her. After another hour, I began to worry. Inca wasn't anywhere to be seen, so I organised a small search party and we spread out across the island to find her.

'INCA!' I yelled, with increasing concern.

It was so out of character; she had never wandered off like this. Despite being on an island, my mind began to wander. What if she had fallen into a ravine or been swept out to sea?

Daylight was beginning to recede, the light was failing and night was approaching. She'd been missing for several hours now and I had no lead on where she might be. I walked further and further from our little settlement. Still no sign. My heart began to race with panic. It was the first time I really understood what this little dog meant to me. She was my everything.

'INCA!' I hollered. Nothing.

As darkness enveloped the island I reached the old bothy, half an hour's walk from our little community. Bothies are little stone houses dotted across the highlands of Scotland, located in pretty remote spots over the landscape, and can be used by walkers and hikers to shelter and sleep. There in the window I could see a flickering candle light. Someone was inside; it wasn't one of us, so it must be a visitor to the island.

I walked up to the door and knocked gently. 'Hello?' I said as I pushed open the door.

I could hear the gentle hubbub of conversation. A small flame of a fire flickered in the corner and there, in the middle of the room, was the unmistakable silhouette of Inca . . . being handfed Italian prosciutto.

She turned to look at me and then immediately back to the hand that was feeding her.

Once we had made our introductions and I'd explained that the greedy dog at their feet was my dog, the visitors revealed that when they had arrived they found a yellow squeaky lemon at the entrance to the door. It transpired that Inca had left it at the bothy during one of our previous visits and she had somehow remembered and made the long journey back to collect it. At which point she discovered the Parma ham and had decided to stay.

I didn't know if I was angry that she'd disappeared or ecstatic that she had been found safe and well. Dogs have that ability to tug at our emotions. I wanted to be cross with her for the worry and anxiety, but I was so relieved to have found her that it was all forgiven.

And all for Mr Lemon.

Mr Lemon was eventually lost to the ocean, but there lies one final tale – or tail . . .

When we eventually returned to London we moved into a little flat with my sister. We had been there for some time when one day Inca appeared at my bed, wagging her tail furiously. There in her mouth was the unmistakable yellow form of . . . Mr Lemon.

I was flabbergasted. It was a complete mystery – how had he got there? I knew we had long since lost him on the island, so how could he now be here, in a flat in central London? It was impossible. But there he was, in her mouth.

I struggled to comprehend what I was looking at. It was only after I got her to drop it and I had examined it that I discovered what had happened.

One of the castaways, Tanya, knew about the lost toy. On her return to civilisation she had been in a shop and discovered that they sold them, so she'd bought one, popped it in an envelope and sent it to me. Inca had got to the post first. Much to her delight, she had discovered the yellow lemon and quite rightly assumed it was hers!

Inca certainly set the tone for *Castaway*. Marooned on the opposite side of the North Atlantic to her forebears, maybe it was fortuitous that Inca was in her natural element. Maybe it's why she was so at home there, surrounded by rough ocean. Whatever the reason, Inca was my anchor on that island. My leveller. The whole island experience was so overwhelming, but for me, Inca was the consistency I needed.

Castaway thrust me into the public eye and stripped me of my anonymity, so much so that I had suddenly become a household name. But I wasn't alone; it was me and Inca. Every photograph of me from that extraordinary year includes Inca. She became an extension of me. She was rarely far from my side. My loyal companion.

I can still remember my heartache when the time came to leave Taransay. It wasn't just the loss, but also the fear of the unknown. What worried me, too, was how Inca would cope away from the island. It pained me to think that I had to drag her from this dog paradise and take her back to a city.

She had spent the first year of her life in this wonderful environment. She had never worn a collar or been on a lead. She wouldn't remember what a car was or what it was like to live in a centrally heated house. She had adapted to island life; her paws were toughened to the rock and bog, her coat was like a polar bear's, thick and curly to keep out the cold wind. She was a Hebridean dog, not a London one.

There is a photograph that was used on the front page of the *Times* on the day we left Taransay; I have a copy of it hanging in our bathroom. It is of me with three other castaways and Inca. I am opening a bottle of champagne while a helicopter hovers behind. It was the first time Inca had worn a collar and lead, and she had contorted it so it was pulling at her neck. It is a sad photo.

A funny thing happened the day after we left the island – I had a wobble. Freaked out by the strange new world in which I found myself, I woke Inca in the middle of the night, packed her into a Land Rover Defender that had been delivered to the island ready for our departure a few days later, and we fled.

I'm not sure what happened or why I did it. I certainly worried quite a few people, and it even made it onto the news. I was eventually tracked down by a *News of the World* journalist. I don't remember much about those few missing days; it was just Inca and I driving through the Scottish highlands.

The month following *Castaway* was a maelstrom of interviews and TV appearances, and Inca came to every single one. She was even part of a fashion shoot for *Vogue* magazine. When I was a guest on *So Graham Norton*, Graham pleaded with me to bring Inca. As promised, we turned up together, only to discover that the other guest, Sophia Loren, was absolutely terrified of dogs, so Inca was consigned to her own dressing room throughout.

She came along on photo shoots for magazines like *Heat* and *Hello*. In this bizarre new world, Inca represented consistency. She, too, had experienced that crazy year and now she was with me for the second part of the journey. We were more than just a man and his dog. We were a team.

Shortly after returning to London, I found myself an agent to help me deal with the tidal wave of requests. They had a smart office in Covent Garden and I used to take Inca in with me.

'Is that the famous Inca?' asked a pretty woman one day,

who was holding a young child's hand. 'Can I introduce my daughter?'

'Sure,' I replied with a smile. It was only later that my agent pointed out that Inca had just been cuddled by Kate Winslet and her daughter. Not bad going for a *Castaway* dog.

Soon after this I met with the then-controller of the BBC, Lorraine Heggessey, who took me to lunch.

'You have a dog,' she said, 'and you seem to love animals. Would you like to present some shows about them for us?'

Apart from being an offer I couldn't refuse, it was proof that Inca had helped me get a job. I have often wondered if I would even have been noticed on *Castaway* had it not been for Inca. I certainly doubt my career would have taken the twists and turns that it has since without her.

Just a month after leaving the island, Inca was packed into a crate and sent by plane to Southern Ireland to help me film a *Holiday* show for the BBC. It was a feature on fly fishing, and together we explored the Connemara coast. It was the start of many, many filming assignments together. During our shared career, Inca arguably became one of the best-travelled dogs in the United Kingdom; she came to Whitby to make a show about Dracula, where she had a starring role as the wild black dog reputed to have run up the steps and into the church. She came to Scotland to make films about dog mushing and the Loch Ness Monster. She came sailing with me around the Cornish coast, and she came along to the World Stinging Nettle Eating championships.

A year after I left Taransay, I was asked to make a *Countryfile* special about the island for the BBC. I was working on the rural affairs show at the time and Inca had become a regular fixture.

We drove up to Inverness in our old Land Rover Defender, where we caught a helicopter to the island. Not for the first time in her life, Inca found herself tucked between my legs as we flew low over the stunning Scottish highlands en route back to the island.

Some people say you shouldn't return to a place in different circumstances; they argue it will never live up to your memories or expectations. For us, it was a little like returning to a ghost town. The pods in which we lived had been removed and all that remained was the skeletal structure of the once-thriving village. What was more heartbreaking, though, was how easily Inca settled back to island life. She remembered every break in the fence, every gate and door. Not only did she look comfortable, she was so happy. Her tail wagged uncontrollably as she headed straight back to where her beloved compost heap had once stood. I felt terrible for having torn her from this canine paradise to live in the concrete jungle where her life was restricted to a small garden and a park. Of course, I know that is a simplistic and unfair portrait of an urban dog's life, but that was how it seemed as I watched Inca bound across the wide-open spaces of Taransay.

We spent several days on the island filming, and when it was time to leave, Inca and I volunteered to stay on. I had no idea how we were going to get back to Inverness, and we had very little food, but I didn't want to leave. I felt at home there; just me, Inca and our island. We spent a week there, until our food ran out and we had to start the long journey back across Scotland.

I had a small flat in London with an even smaller garden, but I was spending more and more time away working so it didn't matter. At that time I was making a series called *Animal Park* for the BBC which was based at Longleat Safari Park, in Wiltshire. My co-presenter, Kate Humble, and I shared a tiny cottage on the estate, and it was a perfect place for Inca to spend her days wandering the woodlands and exploring the parklands. The production office was based in a small wooden building next to Longleat's maze, which was surrounded by a fence. There Inca would spend her days, lazing on the lawn, while we went off to film with various animals around the park.

From there Inca could hear the wolves and the lions, but that was nothing compared to the smells that I would come back with. One of my strongest memories of Inca during that time was as we pulled through the gate to the production office to see her sitting on the lawn, waiting loyally.

Of course, like any dog, Inca had a great ability to get me into trouble, but not always in the most obvious ways. Inca became my shadow, a part of me. In the years of so many changes and so much uncertainty, Inca remained a constant. Reassuring and loyal.

Unless you have ever had a dog, it is difficult to explain the unique bond between person and animal. It is one of mutual dependency. If truth be told, I probably relied on her more than she relied on me. She was my crutch in an often wonky world.

My relationship with Inca was far from unique. On the contrary, as we will discover, mine was the simplest and most basic of relationships compared to others who owe their lives to their Labradors.

CHAPTER FIVE

BLUE-BLOODED HOUND

They say dogs look like their owners, but it's more likely that owners look like their dogs. I'm not sure if we consciously choose a dog because it reminds us of our own appearance or personality – it's much more complex than that – but there is something in it.

When I presented Crufts, you could invariably tell what day it was according to the owners. Of course, I'm using broad brush strokes here, but the more preened the dog, the more preened the owner, the softer the dog, the softer the owner, the harder the dog . . . you get my point.

I've lost count of the number of times I've been compared to a Labrador. Let's compare our personalities.

A Labrador is an intelligent breed; they have a good work ethic and steady, even temperaments. Kind, curious and outgoing, they love to explore and they love company.

Loyal, loving, happy. It seems a little too egotistical to describe my own personality, so I got my wife to do it for me.

'Ben is kind, loving, thoughtful, loyal, considerate.' I can add that I love food and a good party.

Hmm. They're her words, not mine. I'll take the ego trip and add some more thoughts about myself.

I love to explore and I'm curious. In fact, the only difference appears to be in intelligence. I'm not that intelligent, though to be fair I'm not sure Labradors are either.

In broad brush strokes I would describe a Labrador as an eager-to-please, smiling, waggy-tailed friend which is exactly the way I'd like to see myself.

Enough about me, though, let's talk about Labradors . . .

A Labrador has an extraordinary sense of smell and can sniff out food from a huge distance. Of course, this isn't a unique trait to this breed of dog, but their love of food puts them at a distinct advantage; where other dogs, blood hounds in particular, have a superior scenting, the Labrador has the distinction of following a scent for their own benefit.

I'd be walking in a deserted park with Inca when she would pick up a scent. She would place her nose close to the ground and sniff deeply. The sniffs would become intense as she lifted her nose to the air to find out where it lead. Then, like a heat-seeking missile, she would place her nose to the ground and gallop towards the source of the scent. Sometimes it would be a tiny piece of ham dropped from a picnicker's sandwich, or perhaps some bread left for the birds, maybe some feathers from a fox kill or even just an old crisp packet. Inca was always able to sniff out food, however small the remains. I've always thought litter pickers should have a Labrador to help them with their work.

Perhaps one of the unique traits that really marks out Labradors from other breeds of dog is their instinctive love of holding objects in their mouths. Socks, shoes, letters, soft toys, cushions, pillows, towels, books, pants, I've been greeted with them all. The key in the door seems to be the command to pick an object up and bring it to the hall. Our chocolate Lab Maggi is never without a tennis ball. Over the years, her teeth have been worn down into the shape of a ball. I've even caught her fast asleep in her bed with a ball in her mouth. I've even been woken in the morning by a happy Labrador holding my wife's bra and my children's shorts. For a Labrador, nothing is sacred but everything is special.

Apart from coating a carried object with a little slobber, a Labrador will rarely damage it. They hold on with great gentleness, being known to have a very soft feel to the mouth, and it is this gentle hold for which they have become coveted hunting and shooting companions, as they are ideal carriers of birds without breaking the skin or damaging the fallen game. A Labrador can carry an egg in its mouth without breaking it.

Labradors are not famed for their athleticism or their sporting prowess, although in the field many are very athletic. On the contrary, the caricature most associated with this breed is usually of a rather rotund dog who has eaten all the pies. It's a fair depiction; Inca loved food more than anything else in life – she would have eaten her own leg if given half a chance – but she also never knew when to call it quits. She was lacking the sensor to tell her when she was full. A Labrador is never full. I've heard stories of Labs that have eaten themselves to death – admittedly I've only ever heard them secondhand, but I've no reason to doubt they're true. Inca once ate a whole marzipan cake – she looked like a walking barrel afterwards and couldn't walk for three days, but it didn't put her off eating.

However annoying such greediness may be, this insatiable appetite is what makes Labradors so very trainable. Offer a Lab some food and they will literally do anything.

Of course, all this is to tar all dogs of this breed with the same, slightly uncomplimentary, brush. There is such a thing as an athletic Labrador – some lines, particularly those bred specifically for their field working skills, are particularly fast and athletic. They can also be further divided by continent. Across the pond, our North American cousins tend to favour a stockier Labrador, but then, everything in America is larger. But in my mind a Labrador's build is roughly divided between working and non-working. House dogs like Inca tend to be a little less athletic than their working brethren.

Yet one of the reasons for the Labrador's universal popularity is the fact that they are equally good as working dogs or as family dogs. Their gentle, eager-to-please temperament means they are great around children and other animals. If I think of Labradors, I think of children. Ludo and Iona used to sit on Inca. They would inadvertently pull her tail and her ears and place their hands in her mouth to examine her gums and her teeth and she would just lie there. I trusted her implicitly with them.

It is perhaps for that reason – dependability – that Labs have become the most popular family pet across the world. In a world where there is so much distrust, a Labrador offers the opposite. It is this unwavering trust that is so appealing.

According to the Kennel Club's Labrador Breed Standard, the characteristics and temperament of the ideal dog are as follows:

Characteristics: *Good tempered, very agile (which precludes excessive body weight or excessive substance). Excellent nose, soft mouth; keen love of water. Adaptable, devoted companion.*

I would agree on all of the above except for agility. I don't think the build of a Labrador, however trim, is that conducive to agility. When I think of an agile breed, I think of a Collie or a Greyhound – thin, lithe, streamlined and quick.

Temperament: *Intelligent, keen and biddable, with a strong will to please. Kindly nature, with no trace of aggression or undue shyness.*

All true. Labradors are the opposite of shy. It is the one big difference between me and the breed. I am integrally shy. People are often surprised to hear that, but I am not naturally confident.

A Labrador, on the other hand, is shy of no one, although early Labradors were quiet dogs who knew their place because the breeders preferred them to know their place. They are naturally outgoing and will greet all strangers with a pair of socks and then sit confidently next to them. I'm not too sure if this is done in the hope of food and affection or it is simply their nature to please, but it is a universal trait.

Other breeds are naturally more shy. The Greyhound or Whippet, for example, is much more timid.

It is this happy-go-lucky, bouncy, tail-wagging personality that attracts me to the Labrador. In many ways it is the antithesis to the modern world in which we rarely talk to strangers and don't know our own neighbours. Again, I'm talking in broad brush strokes, but generally society has become more cynical and suspicious. When was the last time you said good morning to a stranger on the Tube?

A Labrador wouldn't dream of missing the opportunity to say hello.

Where humans tend to be naturally suspicious, 'why did he just say hello?', 'he must be an axe murderer/mugger/psycho/ nutter . . .', a Labrador will give you the benefit of the doubt. They make the assumption that you are good and kind rather than entertain the possibility that you are bad.

It's an attractive trait. A glass half full; an optimism that is quickly becoming a rare commodity in modern society.

'Biddability' is a word used by many to describe a Labrador. It's an odd word; I don't think I have ever used it before, but I've heard it used countless times by people when describing the humble Labrador. I think it's much more simple; a Labrador is a happy dog, a Labrador always has a smile on its face. They project happiness – the tail wagging and the overall body language project a euphoria that as an owner I find contagious.

I have lost count of the number of times I have returned home after a hard day's work and my spirits are lifted by the tongue-lolling, tail-wagging greeting I receive at the front door. It has also been scientifically proven that stroking a dog can have a calming, soothing effect on people – blood pressure drops with each stroke of the head. Suddenly, all is good in the world.

The easy trainability and superior intellectual capacity of Labradors make them fast at learning tricks and being able to 'perform'. This is why Labradors, as we will discover later in this book, have been trained for all sorts of jobs, from truffle hunters to drug sniffer dogs. It is the combination of all the above traits that makes them so perfect as working dogs.

While Labradors are fun-loving, fearless, often boisterous, and loyal, they can also be quite independent. Interestingly, according to my father, females may be slightly more independent than males.

I have always kept females – or bitches, to give them their correct scientific terminology. In my experience I have found the males to be a little more boisterous. I don't like their habit of cocking their leg to mark their territory, and I have always preferred the slightly more elegant female over the swaggering male. But I wonder now whether my preference is also down to their sense of independence.

Generally, most dog owners stick to the same sex with their animals. I wonder if it's a case of sticking with what you know, or if it is down to the nuanced behavioural differences – because they can be undoubtedly subtle.

Up until maturity, at the age of three, Labradors can have buckets of puppy-like energy which some people misinterpret as being hyperactive. Thanks to their heritage, even the average pet Labrador loves to retrieve things endlessly, obsessively even. Sticks, balls, frisbees, you name it and a Labrador will fetch it.

Inca and I used to spend hours in the game of throwing things. The key was getting her to drop it afterwards, though. Inca would have made a terrible gundog – she'd have eaten the duck.

Labradors sometimes indulge in alarm barking (i.e., they bark at a noise coming from an unseen source), though they are generally not noisy or territorial – unlike a terrier. But because they are easygoing and trusting with strangers, the one job a

Labrador would not be good at is as a guard dog. I used to joke that if a robber ever broke into our house he would be greeted by a Labrador holding an old pair of pants and then he'd be helped by the same eager-to-please Lab, who would most likely show him where all the valuables were hidden, perhaps helping him with the safe and even holding the swag bag to make life a little easier for him. In a Labrador's eyes people are like food. There is no such thing as bad food; some of it, like nuts and bolts or balloons, just tastes a little different, but in the end it's all food.

It was when the Labrador became the fashionable companion to aristocrats with large shooting estates at the turn of the twentieth century that the breed acquired its unbreakable status as a social icon.

On one level, this remains today. A Labrador-owning father of a boy at Radley, a top English public school, joked that parents collect the compulsory black Lab at the school shop when their boys first get kitted out with their uniform. There is indeed this caricature of the green-welly-wearing, Barbour-jacketed, tweed-capped, Land-Rover-driving owner of the Labrador. (I have all of the above, but would never wear/walk and drive them all at once.)

Perhaps it is their aristocratic, Royal-warranted roots that have made them a middle- to upper-class icon. *Tatler* magazine recently did an article on new money versus old money, and in it they included a section on the dogs kept by the different sectors of the moneyed establishment. All of them include the Labrador, the only difference being the colour. Old-school, old-money aristocrats were firmly in the black Labrador camp,

A St. John's Water Dog from the late nineteenth century.

Cora. A Labrador Dog (1823). Print after a painting by Sir Edwin Henry Landseer.

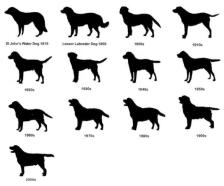

How the Labrador Retriever has developed from the St. John's Water Dog.

The earliest known portrait of a yellow Labrador. Josephine Bowes (1825–74) with her dog by Tony Dury. © The Bowes Museum, Barnard Castle, County Durham, UK/Bridgeman Images

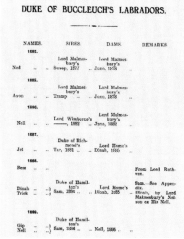

Stud Book of the Duke of Buccleuch's Labrador.

The first registered yellow Labrador, Ben of Hyde, was born in 1899 at the kennel of Major Radclyffe.

Early depiction of Labradors: *After the Shoot* (1895) by William Woodhouse. © Bonhams, London, UK/Bridgeman Images

Betty, a Black Labrador (1911) by Evelyn Blacklock. © National Trust Photographic Library/ Bridgeman Images

Lady Howe's kennels were famous all over the world in the early twentieth century. Her Labrador Retrievers were successful both in the show ring and at field trials. (Photo by Thomas Fall)

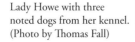

Lady Howe with three noted dogs from her kennel. (Photo by Thomas Fall)

Ch Ilderton Ben, owned by Mrs Quintin Dick (later Lady Howe), in about 1914. He was described as an exceptionally good-looking dog, with a good head, typical of the Labrador breed. (Photo by R. Anderton)

The Duchess of York (later Queen Elizabeth The Queen Mother) and Princess Elizabeth (now The Queen), photographed at Glamis Castle in Scotland with their Labrador Glen by The Duke of York (later King George VI) in 1930. © Royal Collection Trust/ All Rights Reserved

A family surrounded by their Labradors in the garden of their Cambridgeshire home in the early twentieth century. (Photo by Compton Collier)

Two of King George VI's Sandringham dogs, shown at Crufts in 1938.

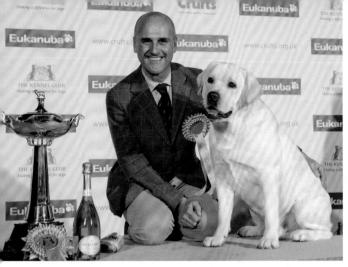

The Crufts Reserve Best in Show title 2013 was won by Labrador Retriever Romeo, owned by Franco Barberi from Cesara, Italy. © OnEdition/The Kennel Club

Before my Labrador years: with my Golden Retriever Lexington.

A Labrador Retriever living up to half of its name. © Eddie Keogh/Reuters/Corbis

Downton Abbey Labrador Pharaoh with Hugh Bonneville. © AF archive/Alamy

Bouncer from *Neighbours*.

Writer Ernest Hemingway in Sun Valley, Idaho with his Labrador Retriever in 1939. © Bridgeman Images

Allen Parton, who was seriously injured while serving in the Gulf War, with his devoted Labradors Endal and Endal Junior ('EJ').

Black Labradors trained as search dogs for the Fire Brigade. © John Daniels / ardea.com

David Blunkett, at the time British Home Secretary in the early 2000s, introduces his then new guide dog Sadie (right) to his previous guide dog Lucy (left), who was retiring. © Stephen Hird/Reuters/Corbis

Russian President Vladimir Putin with Koni. © ITAR-TASS Photo Agency/Alamy

Harold Wilson, then Prime Minister, on holiday in the Scilly Islands with his Labrador Paddy in 1975. © Trinity Mirror / Mirrorpix / Alamy

US President Clinton and his family with Buddy in 1998. © White House/ National Archive/Corbis

Daisy, a Medical Detection Dog. © Andrew Crowley/ *Telegraph*, Camera Press London

Labradors at war. The Normandy Landings, 1944: (Above left) A sapper of No. 1 Dog Platoon, 277th Field Park Company, Royal Engineers, with his dog Nigger, Bayeux, 5 July 1944. The dogs were used to hunt for mines, especially the all-wooden 'Shoe Mine' which was otherwise undetectable. (Above right) A sergeant of the Royal Army Veterinary Corps bandages the wounded ear of Jasper, a mine-detecting dog, Bayeux, France.

Bobs, serving with No. 1 Dog Platoon of the Royal Engineers, locates a buried mine at Bayeux, France. (Photos © Imperial War Museums)

Police training dogs with their handlers at 23rd Battalion Madhya Pradesh Police Dog Training Institute in Bhopal, India. © Sanjeev Gupta/epa/Corbis

Labradors at war. Tracker dogs in Vietnam in 1967. © WS Collection/Alamy

Police officers in Hyde Park, London, on patrol looking for people in possession of cannabis with a sniffer dog. © Mim Friday / Alamy

Two women police dog handlers with drug sniffer dogs, Met Police, London. © Metropolitan Police Authority / Mary Evans

RAF Wing Commander Guy Gibson with his black Labrador dog Nigger and the rest of the crew in 1942. © Daily Mail/Rex/Alamy

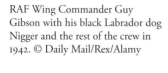

Ben and Inca (as a puppy).

Ben with Inca on Taransay (during *Castaway*, 2000).

while the middle class was placed with the yellow and the new money with the chocolate Lab.

It's a simple generalisation, but while it's true that no stately home would be complete without the obligatory Labrador, these dogs do span the socio-economic spectrum.

Of course, as I've already mentioned, it was the obvious versatility of the breed as a working dog that made its appeal universal to people in all walks of life. In the world of gundogs, a gamekeeper was as likely to have had a prized Lab as was the lord of the manor. Looking back at its origins, you have to wonder how one type of dog could be so adept at such a wide variety of jobs, be capable of working under very harsh conditions and also have one of the friendliest, most affectionate personalities around. Labradors have been valued equally by rough and often seedy sailors and by the grand landowners who refined and preserved the breed in the nineteenth century. It's not one man and his dog; it is everyman and his Labrador.

Snob appeal for Labs came via gundog circles. By the time *The Official Sloane Ranger Handbook: The First Guide to What Really Matters in Life* by Ann Barr and Peter York was published in 1983, Labrador ownership was deemed a badge for a particular social type. The handbook dissected the Sloane Ranger lifestyle through a portrait of the archetypal Henry and Caroline, and the Labrador features large in the section on The Sloane Dog:

The faithful Labrador. Sloane children have all the usual pets – hamsters, gerbils, guinea pigs, tortoises, cats, white mice – but the mark of a Sloane is a Labrador. The noble yellow fellow (or big black beautiful blackamoor) is Caroline's secret love, the one she can give all her thwarted affection to, the one whose smell she dotes on, the one she knows naps on the beds and hopes Henry won't catch.

It is a myth that Sloane Labradors are well-trained shooting dogs. Three-quarters of them are the indulged squire of the woman of the house, dangerous on even a country road, won't come to heel, and roam (males) when there's a bitch on heat, or just because they feel like it.

A few even steal, making off with the first course while the guests are having cocktails. ("The sloberador has eaten the game terrine!"). Sloanes are amused by their own and their friends' dogs' naughtiness . . .

In the United States, too, the Lab attained 'must-have' status, a position which in itself breeds admiring, affectionate and teasing portrayals of dogs and their owners. One of the most popular posts on a satirical website called thedogsnobs.com (whose bloggers bill themselves as 'canine specialists with a passion for judging others') sums up the good, the bad and the ugly aspects of the Labrador Retriever.

We've been harsh on Labs in the past, we can admit that. We may have called them dumb, over friendly, oafish. There is no denying it, though, America loves them. They've been the number one breed in America for . . . a long, long time.

The Good:
1. *Labs are genuinely nice dogs. The vast majority of the time, they're pleasant to be around. They're that iconic bro dog, sort*

of easy going but ready to go when you are. They make great exercise partners, love to play fetch and they can be great family dogs. They're pretty much the dog everyone thinks about when you hear 'I want a puppy' from the mouths of children. For an active family or individual there is a Labrador for all seasons from the heftier plough horse Labradors to the sleek seal-like field-breds.

2. *If you want a general bird-retrieving buddy, there's no reason to look any farther than a good Lab. Even the worst bred among them still has that instinct, even if he's destroying what passes for his hips doing it. We're kidding. Labs actually have better hips than a lot of breeds, but given the sheer number of them out there . . . Good luck telling that to your vet. There's a reason the go-to dog for most hunters is a Lab. They do the job, they do it well and they do it with a good attitude.*

I love the idea of the 'bro' dog. I'd never thought of them like that. The Labrador had always been a loyal companion, but the idea of a 'bro'?

It's true. A bro is someone as happy to go for a muddy run as they are to chill on the sofa. A 'bromance' is one in which there is mutual respect without the emotional ties that often come with a relationship between the sexes. There is very little confusion when it comes to a 'bro'; it is a straightforward, uncomplicated friendship.

This is exactly the relationship I have had with my dogs. There is rarely confusion or misinterpretation. There are no arguments, there's no sulking, no jealousy or suspicion. It is as simple and honest a relationship as you could get.

It's true, too, what they say about hips. *Everyone* will tell you that a Labrador has bad hips but I have never experienced one.

The Bad:

1. *Popularity comes with a price. See the above-mentioned lousy excuse for hips. Also, do us a favor. Open a new tab. Go to your local shelters page. Now look at the breeds. How many of those are Lab mixes? Hell, how many of those are purebred Labs? The shelter is overrun with black Labs and mixes. Indiscriminate breeding has been hell on the breed. If you just want a companion, please do not pay $300 via Paypal for a 'purebreed Silver Labrador'.*
2. *We did call them dumb, yes. Really, though . . . it's more . . . oafish. Herding dog people may find this particular quality more obnoxious than others. Labs assume everyone is their best friend and it can get them in trouble, most notably with other dogs but also with cows, vehicles, electric fences and car interiors.*

True enough. They *can* have bad hips and yes they do want to be everyone's friend – but that's the quality I like in them (well, not the bad hips!). Inca was indeed once zapped by an electric fence, nearly trampled by a cow – and a horse – and been bitten by 'less-friendly outgoing' dogs, all in her unfailing trust and confidence that everything in the world is equally good, happy and safe. That's what makes their behaviour enchanting. If they were just nice, they'd be like the Canadians.

The Ugly:

1. *This is the part where we talk about breed splits again. Labs are the original split breed. You have your blubbery show-line*

Labs that can sort of waddle around the ring, you have you crazy high as a kite field line Labs that are like living with a Border Collie with an oral fixation, and then you have something in between that is mostly produced by BYBs, and that's the Lab that lives in most of America's living room.

2. *There's a solid chance your Lab will eat your house in the first two years of his life. Seriously, they are notoriously naughty puppies who must taste everything . . . and we mean everything.*

All true once again. Inca destroyed everything when she was a puppy. In retrospect, it was lucky I was living on a remote island in the Outer Hebrides for most of her 'chewing phase'.

So the love affair with these dogs is about far more than just social status. The point is that the presence of a loyal and friendly Labrador adds warmth – heart, soul and wagging tail – to any home, even a large, draughty stately home.

Having said that, Labradors really are the aristocracy of dog breeds, for Labradors and stately homes go together like Jeeves and Worcester. According to Simon Jenkins, the former Chairman of the National Trust, there should be a compulsory Labrador in the front hall of every National Trust house. Indeed, he once quipped that he would leave money in his will for a Labrador and a pushchair for every Trust property 'to give the illusion that the family are still in residence'.

A lovable dog known for its quiet obedience, trotting at the heels of an estate owner, also projects values of decency, decorum, status and order. When the global luxury Four Seasons Hotel brand opened a country-house resort in a Georgian manor house in Dogmersfield, Hampshire, the finishing touch to the lavish refurbishment was the arrival of a black Labrador puppy called Oliver Beckington, named after two bishops who once lived on the estate. The hotel has been done up as the ultimate English country estate with an equestrian centre and outdoor activities such as fishing, shooting and falconry. A welcoming dog with wagging tail completes the ambience and makes guests feel at home, part of the family. Oliver Beckington is ranked number one of worldwide guests' favourite thing about the hotel in their comments book.

The Labrador is still a fixture of the seated stately homes of Britain. Over the best part of a decade I filmed at Longleat, in Wiltshire, the seat of the Marquess of Bath. Lord Bath may have a reputation for his renaissance, liberal approach to life – and love, with his wifelets – but his true 'mistress' was his beloved dog Boudica, or 'Boudy', the yellow Lab. He loved that dog. You always knew where Lord Bath was as Boudy was never far from his side, leaving a trail of destruction in her wake.

The housekeepers would follow the pair around. It reminded me of that scene from *Mary Poppins* where they brace everything in the house in preparation for the daily cannon explosion. The housekeepers and stewards would cling on to the priceless vases as the pair tore through the house.

For dramatists such as Julian Fellowes, casting a dog in a period drama ticks lots of boxes. In the case of *Downton Abbey*, the Earl of Grantham's Labrador is an iconic canine: a social symbol, a canny plotting tool and an emotional touchstone. Just as Hollywood movie industry veterans swear by a 'save the cat' scenario early in a screenplay to engage the audience emotionally with a storyline's hero, so Fellowes uses the Earl's relationship with his companion Lab as a siphon for his feelings. The Earl is the sort of stiff-upper-lipped aristocrat whose moods can be better interpreted through the prism of his relationship with his yellow Labrador Retrievers, first Pharaoh, and then, in later series, Isis. A dog is always beside him and features in the show's introduction, walking at their master's heel. The *Downton* Labs are an integral part of the look of the show and of its storyline, and are so popular with viewers they even have their own Facebook account. The page has 5,386 likes, and counting, and is a forum for fans to post sentiments such as, 'Isis is the reason why a lot of us dog lovers watch *Downton* each week – with our dogs!' As Viv Groskop wrote in a blog posted on the *Guardian*'s website: 'She is the queen of the opening shot, the unofficial ruler of the roost and the most loved and consistent character through five long and interminably rambling series of *Downton Abbey*. Forget man's best friend. She is the audience's best friend, the only sane patient in the asylum.'

Groskop was writing about Isis, but the Earl first had Pharaoh. In all, the Earl's two Labradors have been played by three actor dogs. Pharaoh was played by a dog named Roly, who had impeccable thespian pedigree, having come to *Downton* from the set of *Midsomer Murders*. Lady Carnarvon's dog did not like other male dogs in his territory, though, so Roly was replaced by a female dog named Ellie to play Isis. The yellow Lab that took over the part of Isis later, during series three, is named Abbey. Hugh Bonneville, the actor who plays the Earl of Grantham, told me that in real life Isis (Abbey) is 'a moody bitch' on set: 'She rarely comes out of her trailer and demands snacks at all times.'

— * —

A blustery wind battered the trees as the torrential rain enveloped the countryside. Through the course of the car journey, Britain had gone from Indian summer to English autumn. The first of the leaves had scattered the fields as I headed west. I drove through some simple, nondescript gates and into the rolling hills of the estate. Huge oak trees towered above as I made my way along the long windy driveway.

Highclere Castle is an impressive sight. As the fictional *Downton Abbey* it is arguably the most recognisable house in Britain. Even for a relative *Downton Abbey* novice like me, Highclere has a striking familiarity. Whether you have watched the show or not, you will be familiar with the photographs of the iconic building from countless billboards, magazines and posters.

The Jacobethan facade bears a striking resemblance to the Houses of Parliament, unsurprisingly given it was designed by Sir Charles Barry in 1839, following the completion of Parliament. It is certainly a grand building, and even on a rain-soaked autumnal day, it shone like a beacon amidst the Capability Brown-designed gardens.

Most excitingly, it was to here that the 5th Earl of Carnarvon brought many of the Egyptian artefacts with which he and Henry Carter returned from their archaeological excavations – most notably that which led to the discovery of Tutankhamun. The peer would later succumb to the bite of a mosquito, often attributed to the curse of Tutankhamun. While the castle fell into disrepair, it seems to have escaped the curse and survived the years; indeed, the castle has since found fame thanks to Hugh and co.

As I approached up the drive, there, out of the gloom and mist, loomed arguably one of the most famous houses in the world. But of course I wasn't here to see the Egyptian artefacts, or even the *Downton* cast. I was here to meet the real Lords of the manor, the Labradors.

Lady Carnarvon had invited me to tea, to chat about our shared passion for Labradors. She met me at the door with what can only be described as a herd of dogs. A group of Americans were sipping tea in the main hall – one of the upsides of the estimated 150 million worldwide visitors was the increased number of people coming to visit the house. For North Americans, Highclere has become more iconic than Buckingham Palace.

On my arrival at Highclere, there was no doubt about who was boss there. The Labradors marched around the house; 'we had to shut our dogs away when the film dogs arrived,' smiled Lady Carnarvon over tea. When the opening three-second shot of the Abbey's Labrador's rear view first appeared on screens on 26 September 2010, it showed Pharaoh, the first *Downton* dog. But Pharaoh/Roly's problems with Percy, the Labrador belonging to the real-life owners of Highclere Castle, the Earl and Lady Carnarvon, meant he was 'killed off' as a fictional character between series one and two. In keeping with the historical accuracy, the Earl needed another Labrador in series two, which covered the years 1916 to 1919 – for the breed was not only the gundog of choice for the landed gentry at the time, but also fashionably celebrated in the founding by, among others, Lord Knutsford in 1916 of the Labrador Retriever Club. Enter Isis, real name Ellie, and, from series three onwards, the appropriately named Abbie. I love the way the Labs embedded themselves in the affections of television viewers and reviewers. As Viv Groskop wrote, 'As for Lady Carnarvon's Percy, he died shortly after Roly's forced retirement. I make no comment. But we've all heard of the Curse of the Pharaoh.'

They say Maggie Smith gets the best lines, but in the Christmas special of 2011, Isis is central to the plot. Scheming footman Thomas decides to kidnap the Earl's beloved dog, locking her in a woodshed. His plan is to reappear dramatically with her, as her rescuer, just when all hope lost, in a bid to ingratiate himself with the Earl and win promotion to a position as head valet. The scheme hinges, of course, on the Earl's unquantifiable affection for his Labrador. In series five, Isis again wins a good storyline. A visiting art historian played by Richard E. Grant makes overtures towards Cora in full view of Isis, but typically the blinkered Earl sees only advances towards his beloved Labrador: 'Tell your friend Bricker to stop flirting with Isis,' he barks at his wife. 'There is nothing more ill-bred than trying to steal the affections of someone else's dog.'

Despite being a fictional drama, the *Downton* Labrador made front-page news in November 2014. There was speculation that the dog, which had become listless in one episode, was being bumped off in response to discomfort about the dog's name being similar to that of the terrorist group, Isis. This was a ridiculous idea, as the dog was named long before the terrorist organisation began its campaign, in a nod to the real-life *Downton Abbey*'s connection to Egyptology (the fifth Earl of Carnarvon financed the expedition that led to the excavation of the tomb of Tutankhamun in the 1920s). Hugh Bonneville gave a rather more plausible excuse that, according to the chronological time-line, Isis was nearly 30 years old and so therefore his longevity was becoming less and less plausible. But just to show how embedded in the soap opera the whole dog saga is, Hugh Bonneville was moved to post a comment on his personal website: 'To clarify recent speculation, the Labrador that appeared in series one (1912–14) was a dog called Pharaoh. From series two (1916–20) onwards, the Labrador has been a bitch named – in keeping with the Egyptian theme – Isis. Anyone who genuinely believes the series five storyline (1924) involving the animal was a reaction to recent world news is a complete berk.'

So there.

— * —

The Duchess of Devonshire, chatelaine of Chatsworth, is Deputy President of the International Gundog League Retriever Society (IGL) and a long-serving committee member. The IGL organises the Retriever Championship – a three-day event, recognised worldwide by field trailers. The Duchess sits on the Kennel Club's Field Trials Sub-Committee with distinguished names of the gundog world, including Alan Rountree, John Halstead (five times winner of the Retriever Championship), Graham Cox, Joan Hayes and Wilson Young. She is also president of the Yorkshire Retriever Field Trials Society.

According to an article in *Field Sports Magazine*, the Duchess had seven Labradors in training with John Halstead, most of which she brought up as puppies.

The Duchess's late mother, June Heywood-Lonsdale, became a successful field trialler with a rare gift for training dogs, and was a well-known and popular figure on the gundog scene. The

Duchess's own gundog training started with the gift of a Labrador as a wedding present from the much-respected field trial owner Charles Williams, whose trainer Dick Mayall taught her how to get animals to respond on ground near the Duke of Bedford's Woburn estate. She then had further advice from Arnold White Robinson at Stratfield Saye, the home of the Dukes of Wellington.

I was lucky enough to have met the late Dowager Duchess of Chatsworth, Deborah Cavendish, a number of times, too, and we always got on to the subject of Labradors. The first time I met her, I had Inca in tow. The Dowager Duchess doted on her. She wanted to know if I had ever trialled her? She asked if she was greedy, which I took as an insinuation she might be a little 'large' for field work. We both laughed.

The Duke of Westminster also has a handful of handsome black Labradors for when he goes shooting pheasants at his Abbeystead Estate, in Lancashire, or grouse shooting on his Scottish estate, as does the Duke of Norfolk, who keeps a brace of dogs at the family's seat at Arundel Castle, in West Sussex.

The Labrador, it seems, is part of British society, but not just as a status symbol. Pets create a wider family unit, and a Labrador in the picture adds distinctive personality and an extra emotional dynamic under a roof. For me, on *Castaway* all those years ago, the presence of Inca the black Labrador at my side added to my personality. I benefited from her character traits.

A dog is about so much more than just their physical appearance and even their personality. A dog is an extension of you. In the 90s there was a trend towards owning Staffordshire Bull Terriers within urban areas where young people were looking for a dog as a social symbol. A Staffie, which, incidentally, is a wonderful dog and a great family pet, has the reputation for being a tough, muscly, no-nonsense dog. By walking around with a Staffie straining at the lead, the owner was saying 'look at me', 'I'm tough, don't mess with me'. The dog, in effect, was a subtitle for the owner; 'I'm hard', it says.

The same goes for many other breeds. The trend for the Chihuahua (arguably started by Paris Hilton) says I'm dainty, thorough and high maintenance.

A dog is a metaphor for how the owner wishes to be perceived, and the Labrador must surely be the most dependable metaphor for anyone. It is uncontroversial (perhaps the reason so many presidents and prime ministers have chosen the Lab); they say, 'look at me', 'I'm nice'.

It still seems so wildly fantastic that a hard-working, ocean-going, fishing dog from one of the harshest environments on Earth has transformed into such a solid, dependable dog, but again if we think of a solid, dependable, hard-working person, we could do worse than a fisherman.

A fisherman is what I would call a salt-of-the-Earth kind of person. They work hard and toil under difficult conditions to provide fish for our tables. They do it, not for the financial returns, but largely because they love it. They enjoy the ocean, the weather, the outdoors, the land. They are a wholesome bunch, largely unchanged by modern technology. Indeed, the main difference is that boats have become a little safer and they no longer need a four-legged companion.

I would also describe a Labrador as a 'salt-of-the-Earth' dog. The Labrador is 'everyman's' dog. I should probably rewrite that to 'everyperson's' dog. It is the Volvo of the dog world – dependable and arguably a little boxy. And here lies the big question: big or small? Most dog breeds have a pretty standard appearance but Labradors really are defined by their size. It can be quite a controversial topic – opinions on which differ from person to person and also from place to place.

The most important thing to establish is that you should never, ever comment on another Lab's size. It is a subject of much sensitivity. When I visited Newfoundland to establish the early links of the Labrador, I met up with a local Labrador who was something of a local celebrity, used to greet passengers off passing cruise ships as they came ashore.

I'd arranged to meet down by the harbour. A vast pickup truck arrived and out fell Stan. 'Whoa!' I found myself saying uncontrollably, 'He's a BIG boy'. It was as if I had just told the owner that she was fat rather than her dog. She was completely flummoxed and taken aback. 'He is not fat,' she admonished me. 'In fact, he meets the exact breed standards,' she continued. 'He's one of the top dogs in North America.'

That will teach me. It reminded me of the time I mistakenly assumed that a rather famous TV presenter was pregnant. 'Congratulations,' I smiled, pointing to her tummy. 'When's it due?' I asked. 'I'm not pregnant,' she replied, deadpan. I'm going red just remembering it. My point is, never ever comment on girth, be it foetaly or food induced.

Let's be honest, our North American neighbours prefer most things to be a little bigger. I think it is proportional to the continent and its population. Think about it – the highways, the cars, the houses, the portions of food, the chocolate bars, the people, they're all 25 per cent larger. I'm not sure if it's part of consumerism and the American Dream or whether it's something more complex, but let's not kid ourselves, the US of A loves things BIG. Generally I have found that Labradors in North America tend to err on the larger size though the general definition seems to negate this.

Though not an 'official' differentiation, Labs are often given one of two definitions: 'Working' (or 'American') and 'Show' (or 'English').

The terms Working and Show are commonly used and widely known and accepted nicknames in the United Kingdom for Labradors bred either to work at field trials, agility trials or to the gun, or simply to snooze on the sofa dreaming of chasing rabbits. In the United States and Canada, the terms American and English are often used to differentiate dogs that have been bred either primarily for work (the former) or exclusively for companionship (the latter). More confusingly, some Working (or American) Labs enter conformation dog shows, while some Show (or English) Labs compete in field trials and are used for hunting.

Officially there is only one Labrador breed standard, although there are slight differences in permissible heights between the American Kennel Club and (English) Kennel Club standards:

the American breed standard allows a height of between 21.5 to 24.5 inches while the English breed standard allows a height of 21.5 to 22.5 inches.

Apart from this, the two Labrador breed standards are essentially the same. So why do people say there are two types?

You only need to look at Working-type and Show-type Labs side by side to see the differences.

The Show Labs are stockier, heavier and more solid looking. They have wider heads and fuller faces with shorter muzzles, thicker coats, thicker necks, wider, thicker, straighter tails than their Working (or American) cousins and also shorter legs – and hence don't stand quite so tall. Essentially, Show Labs are bred primarily for their looks, to conform to written breed standards. Working Labs, on the other hand, are bred for athleticism.

By comparison, the Working type has a lighter, slimmer-looking body with a more athletic build; lithe and finer boned, they look more agile. The muzzle is sleeker, the face narrower, the coat is thinner, as is the neck and tail, and the legs of American-bred Labs are longer, which is why they can be up to 5 cm taller than English-bred dogs. In combination with their slimmer build, this further adds to their overall look of athleticism. They are the Olympians to their modelling cousins.

Temperament can vary, too, but before I say anything about temperament differences between Working and Show Labs I want to say something about nature and nurture, about what's inherited and what's learned. I don't think you can separate one from the other. When I talk to Lab breeders they tell me that in a litter from Working parents there may be pups with both low and high activity levels, and in a litter from Show parents some pups may pay attention and others can act like hooligans.

Then look at *our* behaviour and how we nurture our Labs. If you're planning to work your dog, and so you get a pup from a Working line, is it not likely that you'll watch its weight more, give it more exercise, make sure that it's fully obedience trained? If that's so, Working Labs might be a bit leaner and more active because that's the way you've raised your dog. That's what I mean when I say you can't really separate nature and nurture; they're embedded in each other.

That said, and talking about populations, Working Labs tend to have higher energy levels and more 'drive' than their Show cousins. They're noticeably more active. The higher energy levels and drive have earned them the label of being more highly strung, as they are always active and need constant exercise and attention. I've met some that behave like Border Collies in disguise. The Working type, and again I'm talking about populations not individuals, is more suited to an active outdoor life than the Show type.

Both types are gentle and kind but Show types are more likely to mature (if any Lab ever really matures) into relaxed and mellow individuals. Show types are probably better for busy families; although still 'driven' and suitable for life as a working dog, if a family pet is what's desired, the Show or English lab is far more likely to slip into this role as they're less demanding when it comes to activity and will more readily chill at your feet at the end of a hard day. Let me put it this way; any young Lab is inclined to have a mad half hour, but when he indulges in these hoolies, it's generally easier to get him to snap out of it if he's from a Working Lab line.

Regardless of type, when it comes to being loving, affectionate and having an immense desire to please, both the Working and Show Labradors are equally matched, and both the Working and Show types share characteristics of being highly intelligent, keen and biddable. (There's that word again!) Bold and confident, they are optimistic and rarely show any sign of aggression towards people.

The reason for the difference between the Working- and Show-type Labs is due to many decades of specialised breeding. Labradors that are wanted for hunting and for competing in field trials are selectively bred for their working abilities; they have higher drive and energy, and are more athletic, slimmer in build and agile dogs. These are the most desirable traits in a Working Labrador. They're bred not to the fickle and ever-changing interpretations of the Kennel Club conformation, not simply to come Best in Show, but to succeed at field trials or retrieving game birds.

Labradors bred for show in conformation competitions are selectively bred for their looks and temperament alone, with the Labs most closely matching the judge's interpretation of breed standard, winning awards in the ring, going on to be used in breeding programmes. Their ability to perform in hunting and field trials is secondary, at best.

In dog shows there's also an interesting compromise between Working and Show dogs. At combination shows, a Labrador's conformation and working ability are equally important, with breeders aiming for the prestigious 'double champion' – Labs that can win in both the show ring and out in the field.

For a shooting or hunting companion, the Working or American Lab's your dog, but if it's a family pet you're after, I'd argue it's a Show or English Lab all the way.

In the United Kingdom most of us want well-rounded family dogs, and what's better than the happy and loyal Labrador? The ideal family pet. I hate the name pet; a dog is so much more complex than that, but it is probably the best way to explain the differences. A pet is more often than not indulged, and if it is not indulged, then it certainly likes to indulge itself. As we know, the Labrador's appetite is legendary and, by and large, family or house Labs tend to be a little more indulged. Some people mistake it for love, but there is no love in overfeeding your dog – it only leads to an early onset of arthritic pain. We all do it, though. We cave into those pleading eyes. The eyes. Those laser beams that say 'put the digestive biscuit in my mouth'.

If we look at the historical provenance of the Labrador, it seems they began life as slightly more lithe dogs, capable of leaping overboard and being hauled back on by the fishermen. Their dense, waterproof coats protected them from the freezing waters, but as they have evolved, so too has their shape. As they became shooting dogs, they needed more power in their hind-quarters.

Whatever the shape, I have learnt you should never comment. Just assume that it is genetics and smile approvingly. Personally, I have always preferred a slightly stockier look. Inca was stocky. Perhaps that is a little unfair – she was solid.

The most important aspect of a Labrador's personality is that it 'needs' a job. That doesn't mean in a hunting/shooting/fishing/ life-saving kind of way. It needs to have a role. How many of us have been 'mouthed' by our Labs. This 'mouthing' is a form of work. They are merely doing what they have been bred for . . . to carry things. If they can't carry a duck or a fish they will make do with a shoe, a pair of socks or a bra. Failing all of that, they will try to carry us. I have lost count of the number of objects I have pulled from Inca's bed over the years. She was like a canine hoarder. It's blood instinct.

Many dog behaviourists will argue that the obsessive chewing displayed by Labrador pups is a result of being 'unemployed'. They need a job; it's the reason Labradors have excelled at so many roles over the years. Inca used to creep up to the children's bedroom at night to be close to them – it was as if she knew that her job was to protect them. Pat White, the animal behaviourist, explained to me that all dogs need a role, but it is a Labrador's diligence that ensures that if they aren't given a job, they will find one. So Inca became the children's nanny, although I've no doubt it might have also had something to do with the trail of food that follows a young child. Inca would often relieve them of their biscuits, sandwiches – and even ice creams.

It isn't just the body that is affected by the size of the Labrador. Size can completely transform the appearance of their face. The nose of a Labrador is one of its most defining features, which can broadly be described as wide or snipey. To my eye, the long thin noses have always looked a little wrong, but what do I know?

The colour of a Labrador is also an emotive subject for the loyal Labrador aficionado. The three recognised colours are black, yellow and chocolate. A little like the shape and size of a Labrador, opinions on colour can be broadly attributed to the various owning communities. Notably, some within the hunting and shooting world feel that the black dog was the original colour, perfect for blending into most landscapes and therefore the most suitable colour for working. Although I can see the logic to this I have also seen plenty of all three colours on estates across the country.

There has long been a debate as to whether different-coloured Labradors have different temperaments. Some theorise that yellow Labs are lazy, chocolate Labs are hyperactive and that black Labs make the best hunters. There's just about as much logic in that as there is in saying blondes are ditsy and brunettes are studious, though.

There is a commonly held belief that a Lab that has any mismarks, brindling or mosaics of other colours represents a non-purebred mixed Lab, but, again, I'd dispute this on the grounds that there are plenty of Labradors with white patches. Even the Kennel Club accepts patches.

Jack Vanderwyk has been able to trace the origins of all chocolate Labradors to just eight bloodlines. Although the colour was not recognised until the twentieth century, these bloodlines go back to 1880, to Buccleuch Avon and his sire and dam, Malmesbury Tramp and Malmesbury June. It is, as we say, a small world.

Recently a new colour has become fashionable, although as old as the breed: Red, or 'Fox' as it's now usually called, which is a dark variation of yellow. They fetch a premium over all other colours. (I saw the reverse happen with Golden Retrievers, the dogs I grew up with. When I was a child, most Goldens were the colour of honey. In fact, that was the name of my family's first Golden Retriever. Today, as a consequence of which dogs win at conformation dog shows, most Golden Retrievers are as white as driven snow.)

I will admit to a bout of excitement when I first heard about the possibility of a red Labrador. The reality is a little less red as it is golden. To my eyes they are merely Labradors that look like Golden Retrievers.

I have also heard of black and white Labradors with Dalmatian spots, but more controversially there is the Silver Labrador. The colour is much the same as that of a Weimaraner; indeed, it is thought that the genes that produced the silvery coat originated from cross breeding. No one is really sure how the Silver Labradors have evolved; it may have been due to a spontaneous genetic mutation or outbreeding.

A little like the Red Labs, Silver Labs command a premium on the market; however, a great number of breeders have complained about the Silver Labs and the internet is rife with 'Say No to Silver' campaigns. But why the controversy? Surely all breeds had to begin somewhere? Well, some say that pedigree Labrador breeders are worried about the competition, but I suspect this is not often the case. However, most pedigree breeders are very committed to the concept of closed registry breeding and are angry that what they believe is most likely to be an outcross has been sneaked into the breed dishonestly. As they are in favour of a permanently closed register, they object strongly to what they see as tampering with tradition and the contamination of the Labrador genetic pool.

With so many concerns being raised over the last few years about closed registry breeding this is a contentious subject with strong opinions on both sides.

Perhaps of more concern to the average pet owner, though, are issues of inbreeding in silver Labradors. In order to establish their Silver lines, breeders will have had to breed quite closely, so it would seem likely that the silver Labrador gene pool is very small. On this basis, accusations of inbreeding in Silver Labs may be well founded, and of course inbreeding increases the risk of health problems arising or becoming exacerbated. However, I'd argue that this is a trans-Labrador issue, not one restricted to Silvers.

Ultimately, though, what colour you choose comes down to personal preference. Each to their own. Unless it involves the Kennel Club . . .

This leads us to an uncomfortable topic: pedigree. Not the food, but the provenance of the breed. When I was a small boy, it was all about the pedigree – that is the parentage, the lineage. A quick look through the stud books over the years and it will become apparent that the gene pool of the Labrador, as with many other breeds, has become thinner and thinner, which has inevitably led to inbreeding. It's what we call incest, but it isn't just a case of two first cousins getting together; this is a slow cobweb of interrelations in which the bloodlines have slowly merged, with inevitable health consequences. Hip dysplasia, a loose and painful fit in the ball-and-socket hip joints, and OCD (Osteochondrosis dessicans), where a fragment of cartilage peels away from bone and causes pain in the elbow joint, are common problems that now affect many, many pedigree Labradors.

Some have argued that the genetic 'closed shop' of the Labrador needs to be loosened up, the blood thinned a little, that some healthy genetic variety is added. This has led to one of the most popular changes now occurring in pedigree dogs – cross breeding.

While the Labradoodle is the cross breed that has received all the press, it is far from the only mix to include the Lab. The list of Labrador cross breeds is extensive. The Abrador is an Afghan Hound/Lab, the Boxador is a Boxer/Lab, the Chabrador is a Chow Chow/Lab, the Double Doodle is a Goldendoodle and Labradoodle, the Corgidor is a Corgi/Lab, while the Lab Pei is a Lab and Shar Pei Mix. The Labradbull is a Lab/Bulldog and the Labrottie is a Rottweiler and a Lab. There is the Matador, a Mastiff and a Lab, the Labraheeler, an Australia Cattle Dog and a Lab, a Labradinger, which is a Lab and an English Springer Spaniel, and my favourite, a Wolador, which is a Timber Wolf and a Labrador.

The names are genuinely funny, but are the crosses really an improvement on the original model? I don't think so. Take hip dysplasia, for example. Now that there are enough Labradoodles around to compare the health of their hips to that of Labrador hips, it turns out their hips are worse than those of Labradors. That is because conscientious Labrador breeders worldwide only breed from individuals whose hips (and elbows) have been x-rayed and are shown to be as well made as possible. Labradoodle breeders don't.

There are more than half a million registered Labradors in Britain, and worldwide the estimates range in the millions. They have overwhelmingly topped the most popular breed list in the United Kingdom, United States, Canada and Australia for decades. The humble Labrador is certainly spreading its genes, but what about the future for the Labrador?

The breed has survived and indeed thrived for more than a hundred years, resilient and adaptable. For a breed that has endured for so long, I have little doubt it will continue to thrive and adapt for another century.

At heart I am a Labrador traditionalist. Like an old Land Rover, I love its simplicity. There are no secrets. I suppose on the one hand Labradors and Land Rovers are really quite basic, but on the other hand it is that simplicity that makes them so popular. No hidden catches. What you see is what you get: happy dogs with a strong attachment to people.

The rights and wrongs of continuing the pedigree lines will be argued for many decades to come, and while my brain tells me it's wrong to encourage and support the pedigree spiral, my heart still wants the classic Labrador.

CHAPTER SIX

ROCK AND ROLLOVER

Inca and I became one. We were always together. Like Ant and Dec, we were a unit.

I lost track of the number of photo shoots we appeared in together. It must have been hundreds over the years, but there was one that stands out for all the wrong reasons.

The late Lord Lichfield had asked if I would take part in a calendar for a dog charity. I naturally agreed, and Inca and I duly visited his studio in west London where he took a series of portraits of the two of us. I was away in Canada when I realised something was wrong. I was up in a remote corner of Muskoka, on one of the many lakes in north-eastern Canada, with one of my great friends, Jake, and although mobile coverage had been limited, I had found a good location for a signal and switched my phone on one morning and it went ballistic. It beeped and beeped and beeped. Text message after text message and voicemail after voicemail. My heart sank. Something terrible must have happened. Someone must have died. My heart raced and I felt sick. My voicemail had more than 80 messages – another message from my network provider informed me to call them immediately as they couldn't cope with the volume of calls and messages.

What on earth had happened?

I picked up the first message. 'Hello, Ben Fogle,' said a female voice, before breaking into laughter and then hanging up. The theme of messages continued in a similar vein and it took some basic detective work to get to the bottom of the mystery.

Unbeknownst to Lord Lichfield, hidden under the voluminous black fur of one of the photos, scrawled across Inca's tag, was my mobile phone number. When viewed on a small contact sheet it was unreadable, but when blown up to a full page of a gossip magazine it was there in its full glory. Much to the delight of the magazine's editor, the photo was blown up and published. This was then exacerbated by a mention of it by Simon Mills on Radio 1, which created a mini-avalanche of callers across the country. Thousands of messages later, I changed my mobile number.

Some dogs are plain naughty. Inca was certainly no goody two-shoes, but I do remember a happy, loyal dog rather than naughty one. Of course she had her moments, usually instigated and encouraged by her stomach. There was the time she stole a cake my mother had made for my father. She ate the whole thing. Another time she stole a chicken and a whole family bag of Dime bars. There was also the time when she chewed up the advance I received for my first book, *The Teatime Islands*, and the time she stole someone's pint of Guinness – she sipped half the glass of an unexpected drinker in a pub while he wasn't looking. But by and large, Inca was a pleaser.

As overseas travel became more frequent in my career, Inca had become a firm fixture in my parents' house. To be honest, she was as much their dog as mine. They loved Inca. They had their own dog, a Golden Retriever called Macy, and the two of them spent a great deal of time together.

But not only was I wracked with guilt at my increasingly long absences abroad, I then worried that Inca missed other canine company when I was back at home and she was with me. I liked the idea of having another dog, but the practicality was far less realistic. It was easy to travel with one dog; to stay in hotels, travel on trains and visit friends was relatively simple with a little planning, but even I knew that two dogs would change the whole dynamic, and make life harder rather than easier.

As I mulled over the idea of being a two-dog home, my sister Tamara confessed that she was desperate for a Lab of her own. She often looked after Inca and loved her, so it seemed silly not to breed from her. To share the Inca love. But whom to mate her with? Without Tinder or dating websites it was difficult to know where to begin.

Mating was a subject we had skirted round before, although not in any serious way! Previously, Inca and I had taken part in a doggy speed-dating night. We had been asked by Disney Films to help promote the release of *A Hundred and One Dalmatians* and the idea was an event at which singles and their dogs would meet. The humans above the table – the dogs beneath it. It was a hilarious night, but neither Inca nor I found love.

Mating! It's such an emotionless description, so prescribed.

Not that I had ever really expected Inca to meet a dashing young dog and fall in love, but it seems so mercenary just to choose her suitor and expect her to have his babies, or puppies even. Once again, Dad came to the rescue in the search for a dog in shining armour. He vetted some of his eligible patients and before I knew it we had found a suitable dog and they had been introduced in London's Hyde Park. A neutral territory where they could get jiggy.

To be honest, I couldn't bring myself to go along. It was like sending my own daughter off, and no one wants to think about that. Dad chaperoned her and a week later she was pregnant.

As with so many important moments in my life, I missed the birth. To be fair, I was supposed to be around, but a diving course in Florida for an upcoming BBC project overran and she gave birth to the first puppy as I was about to board my flight home. My parents carefully helped each of her eight puppies into the world. Even so, I was like a proud parent.

My parents had agreed to look after Inca and her litter for the first eight weeks, until they left for their new homes. My sister wanted to take one and the rest were given new homes with friends and acquaintances. It had never appealed to me to 'sell' any of the puppies; I just wanted them to go to loving homes.

For two months my parents' home became the most popular house in Notting Hill, as people flocked to see the puppies.

My mother cried when the first puppy left . . . and the second, and the third . . . until we were left with a little girl called Lola who went to live with my sister. I can't say Inca was as sad to see them go, though. She was finally free of the pain of razor-sharp teeth on her nipples and she had our full affections once again. Despite that, Inca and Lola became best friends. Inca mothered her – she licked her ears clean each time they were together and she looked out for her when they were in the park.

While no Lassie, Inca had attained a reasonable level of celebrity during her life. *Castaway* had made her a household name; she used to receive more post than me from adoring fans during our year of isolation. She received dog toys, bones and even photographs of would-be suitors. One elderly fan knitted her a jumper, while another admirer sent her some winter booties.

During my early career, Inca was a permanent fixture by my side on most of my television work.

She appeared on the sofa next to me on almost every breakfast show and most chat shows. We did photo shoots together for magazines and newspapers, including a cover shoot for *Heat* magazine, which must surely secure her place in the history of canine celebrity.

On BBC's *Countryfile* she sailed the coast of Cornwall and the Western Isles of Scotland. She accompanied me at the Brambles cricket match in the middle of the Solent and at the World Worm Charming championships in Cheshire. She came hound trailing with me in Scotland and lawn-mower racing in Sussex. She flew out to the west coast of Ireland to make a film about fly fishing for the *Holiday* show and appeared alongside Kate Humble and me at Longleat for more than a decade in the BBC's *Animal Park*.

We also presented two seasons of *Heaven and Earth* together, in which we explored everything from mermaids in Cornwall to the Loch Ness Monster in Scotland. She appeared as the canine apparition of Dracula in Whitby, where she ran through a church, and the famous Black Dog in Suffolk. She even appeared alongside me in adverts for P&O and Nature Valley and had a starring role in a *Vogue* fashion shoot.

Perhaps her biggest roles, though, were on *Crufts* and *One Man and his Dog* where, once again, she joined me on the sofa. It is obviously an exaggeration to call Inca my co-presenter, but you must not underestimate her importance as a calming, reassuring friend.

I suppose I shouldn't really be surprised; everyone loves a cute dog, and a Labrador arguably has the ultimate cute factor. But Inca certainly wasn't the first Labrador to become a household name, and she won't be the last.

Think of a puppy – any puppy – and the chances are you'll think of a Labrador pup. They have been a staple of our cultural landscape for decades. They have featured in films, books, cartoons, TV series and advertisements, usually in the role of a solidly lovable, faithful, heart-in-the-right-place kind of character – even as a bit of a goody four-paws (as opposed to a human goody two-shoes). But the absolute game-changer for the breed in terms of cultural definition was *Marley & Me*.

Suddenly the Labrador had Character with a capital 'C'. Originally a pet-owner memoir penned by journalist John Grogan and subtitled *Life and Love with the World's Worst Dog*, the book became an international bestseller and was soon adapted for film starring Owen Wilson and Jennifer Aniston. *Marley & Me* gave the Labrador a personality, depicted ownership of such a mutt as a roller-coaster ride of high emotions and drama, and spawned a whole industry based on cheesy, life-affirming quotes about the newly glamorous emotional dynamic between a pet dog with a 'big personality' and its long-suffering/long-loving family. The book is laced with beautiful quotes such as:

A person can learn a lot from a dog, even a loopy one like ours. Marley taught me about living each day with unbridled exuberance and joy, about seizing the moment and following your heart. He taught me to appreciate the simple things – a walk in the woods, a fresh snowfall, a nap in a shaft of winter sunlight. And as he grew old and achy, he taught me about optimism in the face of adversity. Mostly, he taught me about friendship and selflessness and, above all else, unwavering loyalty.

Animal lovers are a special breed of humans, generous of spirit, full of empathy, perhaps a little prone to sentimentality, and with hearts as big as a cloudless sky.

It's just the most amazing thing to love a dog, isn't it? It makes our relationships with people seem as boring as a bowl of oatmeal.

Give him your heart and he'll give you his. How many people can you say that about? How many people can make you feel rare and pure and special? How many people can make you feel extraordinary?

He taught us the art of unqualified love. How to give it, how to accept it. Where there is that, most other pieces fall into place.

Slightly saccharine, but then, who isn't soft about their dog? The winning theme of the bestseller, however, is best summed up in Grogan's line: '*Dogs are great. Bad dogs, if you can really call them that, are perhaps the greatest of them all.*'

Grogan relates a cameo-filled story about the thirteen years that he and his family spent with their boisterous, neurotic, destructive but utterly big-hearted yellow Labrador Retriever. For a central character that does not speak, Marley – a dog that never acts as expected of him – holds the story well. The tone is one of exasperated hilarity underpinned by deep-rooted mutual affection. It is a charming evocation of the contrast between the problems caused by a lovable, uncontrolled, clumsy dog and the unswerving devotion and love he shows towards his human family. It celebrates the way in which a pet becomes part of a family's DNA. As Grogan and his wife settle into married life, have children and grow older, Marley gradually slots into his role in the family. Their grief when he dies in old age is heart-rending. Grogan later revealed that the eulogy he wrote in *The Philadelphia Inquirer* following Marley's death received more responses than any other column he had written in his professional life.

The book spawned a whole industry of doggy tales, from *The Art of Racing in the Rain* to my own father's *Travels with Macy*, in which he travelled around North America with his Golden Retriever, Macy.

Traditionally in films and cartoons the Labrador was always the good, quiet, dependable dog. In the 1961 Disney adaptation of Dodie Smith's novel *The Hundred and One Dalmatians*, the Labrador tries to protect all the Dalmatians as they attempt to flee from the clutches of Cruella de Vil and her sidekicks, Jasper and Horace. The Labrador is first mentioned by the Collie at the dairy farm, who comments that the Labrador's human is a grocer in Dinsford. When the Dalmatian family (including all 99 puppies) arrives in Dinsford on their hopeful trek back to safety in London, they are greeted by the Labrador, who, keen to help, informs them that his owner has a truck that will take them to London as soon as it is repaired. But almost immediately the three grown-up dogs notice that Cruella, Horace and Jasper are scouring the village for the pups. Cue lightbulb Labrador moment! In their hiding place, Pongo rolls in a pile of soot and gets the idea that this disguise might distract the villains – they can all pretend to be Labradors rather than Dalmatians.

The Labrador confirms this is a good idea. Who could be suspicious of a common old Labrador? After all the puppies are covered in soot, the real Labrador helps Pongo and Perdita escort the puppies to the truck in groups. As soon as the truck is fixed, Cruella discovers the ruse and orders her minions to catch the puppies. The Labrador – a good egg to the end – attacks Jasper and Horace, giving Pongo and Perdita enough time to get in the truck with all of the puppies.

The film worked on the principle that a Labrador is such a trustworthy dog that it would never do anything wrong. It was above suspicion. I'd partly agree with that sentiment, but only until it involves food, in which case a Labrador would happily sell its own tail, or even its mother.

The Labrador gained further traction in popular culture when a particular book was published in the same year – 1961 – as the Disney animated adaptation of *The Hundred and One Dalmations*.

The book was *The Incredible Journey* by Scottish author Sheila Burnford, the children's book which tells the story of three pets as they tramp nearly 500 kilometres across the wilds of Canada in search of their beloved masters. It depicts the hardship and stress of a tough expedition in which the emotional dynamic stems from the unwavering loyalty and courage of the three animals – two dogs and a cat – and the chemistry they have as a trio. The story is simple . . . the animals' owners, a family called the Hunters, have had to leave them for several months over the summer with a friend, John Longridge, because Jim, the father, is obliged to deliver a series of university lectures in England. Longridge himself goes away for a two-week duck-hunting trip, leaving the animals in the care of a drop-in housekeeper Mrs Oakes. Feeling the lack of human companionship, the animals decide to set out to try to find their owners. Mrs Oakes assumes Longridge has taken them with him, so the animals are truly alone as they follow their instincts and embark on their incredibly perilous journey home.

As a unit, they are an appealing gang. There is a young Labrador Retriever called Luath, who, with a rich golden coat and warm brown eyes, is the strong, brave, eager leader of the pack – but really only in the physical sense. As the most recent addition to the Hunter family menagerie, he channels his natural exuberance into a determined path home, but respectfully defers in all matters to the original family dog, Bodger. Again, we see the Labrador as an easy-going dog who instinctively knows his place.

Bodger is an old English Bull Terrier whose full pedigree moniker is Ch. Boroughcastle Brigadier of Doune. His fur is white with a skin-pink tint and his demeanour shows him to be a brave, loyal, determined, stalwart, elder statesman-like companion. At eleven years old, his left eye is nearly blind and he tires easily, but his tenacity remains unquestioned. He bears the hallmark of his breed in being prepared to fight his way out of trouble, but he is very fond of humans, particularly children, and whenever the group comes across humans on their adventure, he uses his charm to get food and affection. He hates all cats except for Tao – the third Hunter family pet – who is a slender, seal-point, blue-eyed Siamese cat who earned his respect by standing up to him when Tao first joined the Hunters as a small kitten. They bond over the fact that Tao, like Bodger, despises other cats; in fact, before Luath's arrival, dog and cat shared many outings, terrorising the other cats in their 'hood'. Tao serves as an interesting contrast to the two dogs. He can open doors; he is hardier and better equipped to survive in the wilderness, and he has no difficulty surviving on his own when separated from his canine chums. The Bull Terrier and the Siamese are described by Burnford – who modelled the fiction on her own pets – as being 'closer than any other cat-and-dog relationship I have ever seen'. The Bull Terrier and the young Lab also enjoy a close relationship.

The tale is set in the north-western part of Ontario, a landscape characterised by isolated farms, small towns and lots of lakes and river formations. The animals have to fend off ferocious feral animals and cope with freezing conditions, hunger and fast-flowing water hazards. Though it has been pigeonholed as a children's story, the book has universal appeal – particularly to pet lovers – and Burnford herself maintained that she did not write it specifically for children. Clever old Disney saw its potential, and in 1963 it was released in movie form. Thirty years later, in 1993, it was remade for another generation and released as *Homeward Bound: The Incredible Journey*. If you haven't read the book or seen either of the films, I'm sure you can guess how it ends . . . Yes, a warm and fuzzy happy reunion of animals and humans – signalled by the Labrador's bark.

I can still remember reading the story as a child. It was the first time dogs were given real, relatable characters. I saw myself in Luath. I empathised with him. It was the first story I read that made me cry.

By the 1990s, the Labrador had achieved such iconic status as a dependable hero that the brown mongrel described by Ludwig Bemelmans in his *Madeline* series, written between 1939 and 1961, was changed to a golden Labrador in the 1998 live-action film adaptation. For those unfamiliar with the illustrated *Madeline* tales, the opening page gives the essence:

In an old house in Paris that was covered in vines lived twelve little girls in two straight lines. In two straight lines they broke their bread and brushed their teeth and went to bed. They smiled at the good and frowned at the bad and sometimes they were very sad. They left the house at half past nine in two straight lines in rain or shine — the smallest one was Madeline . . .

My little daughter Iona and my boy Ludo both love Madeline. Genevieve, the dog, became Madeline's canine saviour and friend in an early adventure. Seven-year-old Madeline, the boldest and most outgoing of girls at her Catholic boarding school in Paris, stood on a bridge over the River Seine to make a speech to the other girls and in her excitement fell into the waters below. She was duly rescued by a stray, Genevieve, who jumps into the river and saves her. Madeline brings her rescuer back to school and hides her. Miss Clavel, the nun who runs the school, says Genevieve must stay in a kennel outside, but Lord Cucuface, arriving for an inspection, says the dog must go because it is against the rules to keep her there. In the course of a subsequent adventure, Madeline is reunited with Genevieve and they become friends.

When Warner Brothers set out to create an animated television series based on the DC Comics character Krypto the Superdog, they chose to depict the main protagonist as a white Labrador Retriever. Clearly we are in the realm of fantasy here. Although Krypto's breed is never specifically described in the comic books, he was drawn as a white dog of generic Labrador pedigree – presumably because he shares Superman's moral values in being champion of good and righteousness in society.

Krypto was originally Clark Kent/Superman's dog on Krypton before the planet was destroyed. Like his superowner, he has the same powers, but, in a nice creative touch, some of those powers are heightened as you would expect in a dog, such as his super hearing and sense of smell.

Sitcom writers, when creating the perfect family or set of families, often fall back on the addition of a fun-loving Labrador as a universally recognised symbol of the ideal domestic quota.

Take the Australian soap opera *Neighbours*. *Neighbours* was a huge part of my childhood, and the importance of the Aussie soap cannot be overstated. At 1pm every day, the whole school would race from lunch to the television room to keep up with the hottest TV show of the time.

There was never any question in my mind as to the real star. It wasn't Kylie or Jason but Bouncer the yellow Labrador. Bouncer added complexity, humanity and bemusement to the plot for six years. From the time he made his first screen appearance as a cute golden-coated puppy acquired from a shelter during an episode broadcast Down Under on 4 February 1987, until the day he left the series, six years later on 12 February 1993, Bouncer lived at three addresses on Ramsay Street, fathered two litters of puppies, survived road accidents, a chip-pan fire and serious mushroom poisoning, and recovered from being lost.

Bouncer was supplied and trained by Luke Hura, who runs a canine actors' agency. Rather amazingly, Bouncer was paid more than the human cast members and his fan cards became the most popularly demanded above any other cast member. At one stage Hura revealed that the dog was worth between $100,000 and $200,000. Thirteen weeks after filming his final scenes on *Neighbours*, Bouncer died of cancer, aged only seven. Following his death, he was sent thousands of tributes from fans around the world.

Bouncer's most famous storyline was bizarre in the extreme, even by the standards of a long-running sitcom. It had Bouncer dreaming that he was getting married to Rosie, the sheepdog that belonged to Clarrie McLachlan next door. During an interview, Anne Charleston (who played Madge Bishop) revealed,

'The whole cast was mortified about that! It reduced it to a three-year-old's programme. It was very strange.' Bouncer's dream was later named the second 'weirdest' storyline in the show's history, though his contribution – as a loyal and loved Labrador friend – was celebrated by critics. Josephine Monroe commented positively of Bouncer in her book *Neighbours: The first 10 years*, stating: 'Bouncer was a hero – he even answered the phone and barked to Joe when baby Sky was in trouble – and often had major storylines of his own like the time he was run over and nearly died. But most importantly, he was a loyal and loved friend.' She also declared him one of the most-loved characters in the serial's history. Celebrating the serial's 25th anniversary, British magazine *NOW* included Bouncer among their profiles of their favourite characters, while Daniel Bettridge of *The Guardian* said the faithful Bouncer was one of the best actors to 'tread the Ramsay Street tarmac'.

In children's television the Labrador again often serves as the most easily recognisable friendly dog. In *Big Barn Farm*, a television series produced for the BBC children's channel CBeebies with a mixture of live action and animation, Digger is one of the four young animals on a farm – the Farmyard Bunch – who share adventures. Interacting with Petal the piglet, Gobo the goat and Dash the donkey, Digger is a Labrador Retriever puppy. He is the youngest of the four chums, cute, naïve and willing to please. Brimming with boundless energy, he is always eager to prove himself and put himself forward for any new jape. He is a tiny bit dim and sometimes slow to catch on, but Digger is never happier than when playing with his friends. His catch-phrase is, 'I can do that! I can do that!'

It is good for the status of the Labrador that one was written into *Lost*, an American drama which followers the survivors of a passenger jet crash on a mysterious tropical island in the South Pacific, and which has been dubbed one of the greatest television series of all time. Vincent the yellow Labrador is the only non-human survivor of Oceanic Flight 815, and his name – from the Latin *vincere*, to conquer – means 'the one who prevails'. The series was broadcast on ABC over six seasons from September 2004 to May 2010 and comprised a total of 121 episodes. In an interview, executive producers Damon Lindelof and Carlon Cuse admitted that at the show's end the only character they could promise would be alive was Vincent. The final shot of the series showed Vincent, alive, lying next to a dying character called Jack. He and Walt were the main characters and the only ones of the original characters not shown to have died by the end of the series. Thus Vincent duly prevailed. Actor Naveen Andrews, who portrayed Sayid Jarrah, joked about his theory that the series finale would feature rescue boats coming for Vincent while the graves of all the survivors were seen behind him.

Each of the episodes featured a storyline on the island with a secondary storyline from another point in a character's life. One of those characters was Vincent, who was travelling aboard Oceanic Flight 815 from Sydney to Los Angeles in the luggage department after moving to the United States with two characters called Walt and Michael. Like all the human characters, Vincent was given a pre-island back story and plenty of on-island storylines which included having as many as four owners, being attacked by a polar bear, revealing dead bodies, and so on. Critics often observed that Vincent was frequently present just before something bad happened on the island.

Vincent was played by two dogs: one a female called Madison (trained and overseen during filming by Kim Stahl) who previously worked in tracking and obedience competitions and made her TV debut in *Lost*, the other a male known as Pono, who was discovered by crew members eating at Marcos' Diamond Head Cove Health Bar. His first scenes came towards the end of the second season, but soon *Lost* fans knew all the Pono trivia. Like every well-bred Labrador, he is especially fond of children and loves water (Pono is an excellent surfer). True to the roles mostly played by Labradors in film and TV, his name means 'righteousness' or 'moral correctness' in the Hawaiian language.

Of course, in the off-screen world of celebrities the Labrador's dependability and loyalty have long attracted a following. Paul McCartney had a 'wild' Labrador that would escape the grounds of the McCartneys' house in St John's Wood, London, and trot out for nights on the town. She gave birth to a litter of black Labradors, one of which the McCartneys named Jet, presumably because of the colour of his coat, and Jet is believed to have been the inspiration for the track of the same name that appears on the iconic *Band on the Run* album that McCartney wrote for Wings in 1973. 'Jet' peaked at number 7 in both the US and British charts in March 1974, although the lyrics bear no relation to canine influence.

It seems Labradors were rock 'n' roll; Keith Richards also had a Labrador that he kept in his house in West Wittering, in Sussex. Richards succeeded in irritating his neighbours not only by often playing loud music throughout the night but also by his inability to keep control of his Labrador, which would regularly stray on to his neighbours' properties.

In the cultural sport known as celeb-watching, fed by the paparazzi, Labradors have often provided photo opportunities for their owners or added to their celebrity aura. Arnold Schwarzenegger, for example, had two Labradors: Gustav (named after his father) and Spunky (I'll let you deduce that one). They formed part of an exotic menagerie which ran to a miniature pony, a pot-bellied pig, a cockapoo and various ducks and rabbits. In 2008, Arnie signed a Bill in the State of California that provides for enforcement of 'pet trusts' that animal owners set up to pay for the continuing care of their pets after they (the owners) have died – thus giving peace of mind to many senior fellow Labrador owners.

Arnie is not the only actor in Hollywood who appears to have fallen for the charm of the Labrador. Kevin Costner is another Hollywood figure well known for his love of dogs. He keeps a dynasty of golden Labradors, the matriarch of which, Rosalita, starred alongside him in the 1989 romantic thriller *Revenge*, directed by Tony Scott. One of her puppies was named Wyatt after the lawman Wyatt Earp whom Costner played in the eponymous movie. Daisy, the third yellow Labrador, arrived in 2000, and later had to be treated for her addiction to chewing furniture and shoes. Sylvester Stallone also keeps dogs at his home in Hollywood, among them a Labrador named Flipper, while Kevin Spacey has a black Labrador cross called Legacy. Frank Sinatra had a Labrador named Leroy Brown, presumably after the 1973 song 'Bad, Bad Leroy Brown' that was the last number-one hit for American folk rock singer Jim Croce before his death – which Sinatra released as a cover version in 1974.

In the circles of literary giants, too, what could be more fitting than to learn that Ernest Hemingway had a black Labrador gundog, or that Roald Dahl, who owned an assortment of dogs, had a black Labrador called Jelly? Of course they both had Labs. Labs inspire.

In the world of still advertisements or film commercials, a Labrador is often used for several reasons. First, the breed is famously easy to train. Second, they are universally recognised as 'a perfect family dog' so by their very presence they signal domestic bliss (and their puppies are indescribably cute). Third, everyone knows the size of a Labrador so if you have one in the back of a new car that is being launched with a pervasive advertising campaign, viewers can instinctively register 'family car with generous-sized boot'. Put a Schnauzer in the back and only a minority would be able to interpret the proportions it represents within a cameo family shot. The other advantage of the Labrador is that, as the number one dog owned in the United Kingdom, the United States, Australia and so on, its appeal reaches a massively diverse ownership. In terms of a 'hearts and minds' strategy, there is nothing so winning as a puppy.

The most famous advertisement featuring the Labrador is, of course, the one that features the Andrex puppy. The appealing playfulness of a young puppy is cleverly engaged on behalf of a brand of toilet roll. The Andrex puppy first appeared in 1972 and since then there have been 130 different adverts featuring the adorable golden-coated individual. In 2004, the company replaced its advertising slogan 'Soft, strong and very very long' with 'Tuggable, huggable softness', and recently changed it to

'Be kind to your behind'. The brand is sold in the United States and Australia as Kleenex Cottonelle, and in Australia the puppy is known simply as the 'Kleenex puppy'. The puppy thus represents softness, strength and a good thing to have as an integral part of your life.

When the first advert was scripted in 1972, the original creative concept was blocked by television regulators as it was thought that the image of a cute little girl running through her house trailing a roll of loo paper would encourage wastefulness. So, in a stroke of genius, the little girl was replaced by a playful Labrador puppy who took the end of the roll in his teeth and ran through the house with it. This was accompanied by a slogan which said, 'New Andrex goes a long, long way'.

The campaign went on to become one of the best-known commercials in the country. The most memorable of these, for most people, was the 'Little Boy' variation of this advert, which showed a young boy sitting on the loo and left without any paper after the puppy has run off with the end in his mouth and is pictured entangled in the roll. In 1991, it was voted the nation's favourite advert. Having featured in more than 100 commercials and as it celebrated 40 years on TV, the Andrex puppy soft toy was released to raise money to support charities including National Canine Defence League and Guide Dogs for the Blind. The Andrex puppy even has a kennel on the internet so that younger visitors can meet the puppy, collect tokens and email comments about their own puppies in the Bark Back section of the site.

As the lifestyle marketing folk have long realised, dogs are a winner – dogs looking cute, dogs doing crazy things, dogs getting up to amusing antics. Their appeal is universal, and to harness that wittily can translate into commercial success. Tap into man's love for his canine friend with an enterprising idea and you don't have to do research on a potential market.

Beyond advertising, it's amazing how much Labrador stuff there is out there. As a Labrador owner there is an assumption that I will love anything with a Labrador on it. Over the years I've been given everything from Labrador tea towels to Labrador notebooks and even a Labrador clock. I suppose their unmistakable silhouette is easy to replicate.

It seems I'm not the only one, though. As the Labrador is the number one choice of dog in so many countries across the world, it follows that there is a huge market for Labrador novelty items. In fact, go to a point-to-point, a three-day event, an agricultural show, a Christmas Fair or a crafts market, and you are sure to find stalls selling everything from mugs and tea towels to upholstered three-seat sofas decorated with Labrador motifs or portraits or silhouettes. Vicky Elliot – who runs The Labrador Company, which sells silhouette clocks with wagging tails, cashmere scarves, bespoke Eaton bags, dog beds, cushions, fabric by the metre, key rings, notelets, throws, foot stools, mirrors, armchairs and ottomans – described one lightbulb moment. 'I bumped into an old friend who told me he now had a chocolate shop in Stow-on-the-Wold. 'You should do Labrador-shaped chocolates,' I said. 'No, wait a minute. *I* should do Labrador-shaped chocolates.' Acting on her idea, she created her distinctive range of boxed confectionery: six handmade chocolate Labradors – two dark, two milk and two white chocolate. 'The perfect little present to make people smile! Belgian chocolate.

Made in England. Fairtrade. For human consumption only.'
Within weeks, she had sold 15,000 . . . 'People can't get enough.'

The Labrador Company also extends to ranges for Spaniels
and Dachshunds, but Elliot, a former Labrador owner, says she
sells more than twice as many Labrador products as those of
the other breeds. She puts this down to the fact that people are
'wet about their dog' and also the fact that, as a Labrador is a
big dog, a Lab owner has to buy into its presence in the family
home and car, and invest in some kit. Her ranges appeal to an
upmarket audience, which extends all the way up to the man
with his customised Range Rover complete with cabinet
marquetry for guns and cartridges in burr walnut and bespoke
travelling space for the beloved Labrador gundogs. But the secret
of success behind all the notable Labrador-themed novelty busi-
nesses is the genuine affection for the breed. Look at one of The
Labrador Company's clocks with wagging tails and you see the
stance is right, the tilt of the head so familiar . . .

CHAPTER SEVEN

THE NOSE KNOWS

Inca helped find me a job, a career and a best friend. However, I'd argue her greatest achievement was finding me a wife.

The Fogles have always walked their dogs in Hyde Park. I love it there; a little bit of the country in the middle of the city. Inca and I would have our hour-long set loop through the park, seeing the same people, but one day I spotted a tall, hot blonde running with an athletic, agile brown dog. She was soon christened 'Park Girl' and I became rather infatuated.

I would look out for her in her familiar red tracksuit. I learnt to recognise the gait of her run from a distance, and Inca and I would redirect our walk accordingly. The problem was that Marina had what I call 'pretty girl radar' and would alter her course to avoid a potential stalker like me.

For more than a year we would watch in awe as this beautiful blonde and her dog dashed across the horizon in a blur. Occasionally our paths would cross and I would get butterflies, but I was always too shy to speak to her. If Inca would only 'talk' to her dog and start playing, then it would be the excuse I needed. The problem was that Inca had never really liked other dogs. I put it down to her lack of socialisation during our year on Taransay.

So one day I set a trap. Inca and I lay in a bush and waited until she appeared. I booted Inca from the bush into the path of her sleek brown dog. Inca growled, the brown dog ran faster, and the pretty blonde carried on oblivious.

In the end it took a chance meeting at a party to finally say hello. Out of her running kit, though, I barely recognised her.

'You're the man with the dog,' she smiled. That smile was so sexy.

I discovered her real name was Marina and that her dog was called Maggi. Maggi had been bought from a rescue centre in Henley and was in fact half-Lab, half-Collie. She was a beautiful dog – fast, agile, sleek and very, very funny.

I like to think it was love at first sight, but it could never be true love until we knew the dogs liked one another. Love me, love my dog. I was terrified that Inca would try to attack Maggi when we first got together, so we organised to meet on neutral ground, the Ladbroke Arms pub in Notting Hill. Apart from a little grumble, they loved each other straight away.

We spent a year going out. The four of us. We would go for dirty weekends to Holkham with the dogs. To Woolacombe in Devon – with the dogs. Our lives and our courtship revolved and evolved around the dogs. All we would talk about was our dogs. When I look back at all our early photographs, they are dominated by pictures of our dogs.

There is one day that stands out, though. It was a watershed. A game changer. To be honest, it was probably the moment when I actually decided that Marina really was *the one*. Apart from my sister and my parents, no one had ever been trusted to look after Inca.

It was a Monday morning and I bumped into Marina running in the park with Maggi. I was ambling back to the car with Inca at my side, 'Why don't I take her with me?' smiled Marina. 'She could come on our run.'

If I'm honest, I panicked briefly. Marina was certainly no stranger but I had never just left Inca with someone apart from family.

'Okay,' I stuttered, and before I knew what had happened, Inca was disappearing into the distance with the blonde park girl and Maggi.

Shortly after I first met Marina, she and her family flew to Mozambique for Christmas, so naturally I volunteered to look after her dog while I was away. I can remember driving down to my parents' house just outside Arundel, in Sussex.

'Who's this?' asked my parents as Maggi marched into the house.

'Oh, just someone's dog,' I replied nonchalantly.

My parents still hadn't met Marina, or even heard about her until now. The first they knew of her was her dog Maggi. At the end of Christmas both my parents confided in me that if Maggi's owner was anything like the dog, she must be pretty special.

Marina returned in time for the New Year and the four of us saw it in at my parents' house, where we spent several days walking along the windswept beaches. It was blissful. I have such

happy memories of those carefree days of young love. And that's
when Maggi tried to commit suicide . . .

As always, Maggi had one of her beloved tennis balls in her
mouth. She rarely left the house without one. We were splashing
around in the surf on Climping Beach, a long pebbly section of
the coast that runs west from Littlehampton. I picked up the
ball and threw it a couple of times, then on the fifth throw I
decided to give it a little more welly. The ball went careering
through the air and over a wooden groyne. Without a second
thought, Maggi bounded after the ball and followed it over the
groyne into the abyss beyond.

My heart leapt. What was beyond the groyne? We had reached
the end of the beach, so I raced to the edge and peered over. It
was a sheer six-metre drop to the river estuary below.

I couldn't believe it. Had I just killed my girlfriend's dog?

'Maggi!' I shouted. 'Maggi! It was a huge drop. The water
was coming in fast and with the rising tide the river was running
wild. Even if she had landed safely she would easily be swept
up into the current.

'Maggi!' I shouted again.

My eyes scanned the water but there was no sign of her. By
now a small crowd had gathered. Alerted by my frenetic, wild
calling, they had gathered by the railing. There was still no sign
of Maggi. Inca pottered around, unconcerned for her new friend.

And then I spotted her, circling in the muddy waters close
to the wall . . . proudly clutching the tennis ball. How on earth
were we going to get her out? It looked impossible. Then I
spotted a small piece of foreshore that had been uncovered by
the tide and, using stones, encouraged her to swim towards it.

Now she was standing on a tiny patch of mud, surrounded on one side by a sheer wall and the other by a fast-flowing river more than 60 metres wide. The tide was coming in fast and soon the little island would be submerged. I thought about calling the Coastguard or the RNLI; they would have to rescue her by boat, I thought, but then a young boy pointed out that there was a form of ladder recessed within the wall. Without thinking, I leapt over the railings and began to descend to the little castaway dog.

The assembled crowd grew a little larger as I reached Maggi. Now how on earth was I going to get her back up? There was only one thing for it. I scooped up the soaking wet, muddy dog and began to climb the ladder.

I'm not sure if you've ever tried to climb a ladder with a heavy weight under one arm and only one hand to grip it, but it's pretty precarious. Maggi weighed 25 kilos, not an easy shape or weight to hold under one arm. I was just grateful it wasn't Inca – there's no way I could have carried her under one arm.

Slowly I worked my way back up the ladder, holding the rusting bar with one hand before taking a step and then letting go briefly to catch the next bar a little higher up. Several were broken or missing, which required a little acrobatics along the way.

I'm not quite sure how I defied gravity, but somehow man and dog made it to the top. There was a round of applause as I placed Maggi, still clutching her ball, onto the ground. If this didn't impress Marina, nothing would. I had just saved her dog. Admittedly, it was my throw that had got her into this situation, but that is a minor technicality.

Fortunately, all was well, and we didn't look back. Our fate was sealed. In years to come we would often joke about the time

I saved Maggi and how it was probably a ploy by the dogs to bring us together.

But while my actions may have looked brave to Marina, it was nothing compared to the actions of working Labradors over the years which have been nothing short of heroic.

Labradors excel as search-and-rescue dogs. A mixture of good scent detection and a desire to work has brought these dogs to the frontline of terrorist activity and natural disasters. Earthquakes, floods, tsunamis, hurricanes . . . the list is long and impressive. Where humans are prone to emotional anguish at the sights they have to deal with, dogs just go to work. They search relentlessly, day and night, for survivors of natural disasters. Then, when all hope is lost, they become cadaver dogs, hunting for the remains of victims.

Rescue dogs not only work diligently and risk injury by going into areas deemed unsafe for humans, but they also offer comfort to their human handlers. It is beyond the scope of this book to celebrate every amazing Labrador tale, but a few serve to highlight the depths of loyalty and ingenuity shown by this breed when faced with a situation in which their master is vulnerable. As one professional disaster-relief dog trainer says, 'You don't have to explain things to a Lab. They just do it.'

The recent conflicts in Afghanistan and Iraq have seen Labradors deployed across the region, creating their own inseparable bonds between soldier and dog. When Marine Pfc Colton Rusk was stationed in Afghanistan he shared a cot with his beloved dog Eli. On 6 December 2010, the day that Rusk was shot and killed by Taliban sniper fire in Afghanistan, the dog had just located IEDs (Improvised Explosive Devices) but couldn't protect his master from three Taliban bullets. When Pfc Rusk fell to the ground his dog crawled on top of him to shield him.

Rusk's family decided to adopted Eli after the tragic events in Afghanistan – he had loved that dog and his family wanted their son's legacy to live on. Eli was the second dog to be adopted by a fallen service member's family, and emotions ran high at the official repatriation. 'We're going to share the love that we have for our son with something he loved dearly,' said Kathy Rusk. 'It had given me some comfort knowing Colton wasn't alone over there. Colton would have loved knowing that [we were adopting Eli]. Like he used to say, "what's mine is his". We're Colton's family, so now we're Eli's family. [The adoption process] did get our minds off the sadness.'

The story makes my heart skip. Poignant and moving, but to anyone who has loved and been loved by a Labrador, completely relatable.

Military statisticians claim that as many as 2,700 dog teams have been in action as sniffer dogs in Iraq and Afghanistan at one time, many of them Labradors. As General Petraeus, the US Commander in Iraq in 2008, said, 'The capability the Military War Dogs bring to the fight cannot be replicated by men or machines. By all measures of performance their yield outperforms any asset we have here in our inventory.' The high regard with which the US military regards Labradors was again made clear in February 2010 when the *Wall Street Journal* reported that the US Marines shot a farmer's dog which was acting aggressively towards an explosives-sniffing Labrador. This was because they could not afford to have the valuable asset maimed or injured. 'We consider the dog another marine,' was the official line.

Dogs are used by the military for vigilance, protection, pursuit, and search and rescue, but mainly for detecting the scent of homemade bombs. Improvised Explosive Devices are responsible for the deaths of more than half of the coalition troops killed in Iraq and Afghanistan. When war dogs are in operation, the IED detection rate rockets to as high as 80 per cent. No form of technology is more efficient than an eager-to-please, non-aggressive, strong-nosed dog.

The Labrador's independent nature enables it to work off the lead, which keeps the handler a safe distance from hidden bombs. The handler keeps control with voice and directional commands and reads the dog's body language in order to raise an alert, and the trackers can pick up a scent and follow it back to the bomb's delivery boy. Dog and handler live side by side; the dogs endure the same conditions as their handlers and receive treatment for Post Traumatic Stress Disorder (PTSD) as and when it is required. They even wear tactical body armour and flak jackets to protect their vital organs. In sensitive situations that are deemed unsafe for humans to operate in, a dog can go in wearing a flak jacket fixed with a wireless camera and speakers so a handler can see what the dog sees and instruct it by audio command.

The fate of dogs in war is largely unreported; many survive to work on repeated deployments, but some are killed in action or suffer Post Traumatic Stress Disorder. The story of Corporal Kory Wiens from Oregon and his MWD Cooper, a four-year-old golden Labrador, stands out as a poignant reminder of the risks that dog and handler run in the course of duty. The close pair were killed together by an IED while patrolling in Iraq in 2007. Wiens had planned to adopt Cooper when the dog retired at the age of eight or nine, and when Wien's family received his personal effects, they were moved to unpack a large number of Cooper's dog toys. Their ashes are buried together in Wiens's home town and their story caught the imagination of animal lovers. A dog park at Fort Carson, outside Colorado Springs, is also dedicated to commemorate the duo.

The story of Gunner, a golden Labrador diagnosed with the canine version of PTSD, is an example of the incredible bond that can develop between man and dog. In 2004, an American couple, Deb and Dan Dunham, lost their son Jason to an insurgent's grenade in Iraq. Their process of grieving and healing came after they adopted an injured bomb-sniffing dog that was haunted by war, and also called Gunner. The process of healing on both sides is slow but steady. As Dan Dunham says, 'Everybody's resilient – human and dog', whilst acknowledging that he and his wife can't heal all of Gunner's scars any more than they can forget their own grief. Dan's sentiment sums it up. 'To us it's like Jason died yesterday. To Gunner, whatever happened to him – it's probably like that happened yesterday. We get up each day and find a new way to get through the day, realising that Jason's not here. We have to pass that on to Gunner.'

From the tough, dangerous life of hardship and treacherous insecurity, incredibly heart-warming stories emerge. In 2008, Sarbi, a Labrador/Newfoundland cross who worked as an Australian Special Forces explosives detection dog, went missing in action. She was caught up in a battle with the Taliban when a rocket-propelled grenade exploded close to her, injuring her handler (among a group of eight other soldiers). The force of the blast broke the lead that attached her to her handler's body armour and, in the confusion that ensued, she was nowhere to be found. She remained 'missing in action' for 14 months. The Australians kept reminding other soldiers of their loss and asked them to look out for her. Eventually Sarbi was spotted by an American soldier with a local Afghan man who was aware that the Australians were missing a dog. Sarbi was then liberated and flown by plane to be reunited with her Australian handler.

There are more . . .

Tangye, a black Labrador bought as a puppy by a British soldier from a dam worker in Afghanistan, became a camp mascot, patrolling alongside the soldiers for five years. Named after a village on the Helmand River lying opposite the forward-operating base at Kajaki, Tangye was 'fearless under fire' and would be the first to jump through a hole if soldiers blasted one into a compound wall while they cleared a village of insurgents. L/Cpl Meheux, a 44-year-old Territorial Army soldier, said Tangye had done more patrols than most soldiers and he should be honourably retired to keep him safe. 'When the lads are under contact (fire) he will run up and down the line barking and wagging his tail. It's as if he is shouting encouragement – he loves it. But we had to stop him coming out on patrol about a week ago. The IED threat is just too high. It's gone through the roof. The Taliban probably know about him and think he is a sniffer dog. I'm sure they would want to make him a target,' L/Cpl Meheux said. 'He has been such a morale-booster for the lads. It would mean an awful lot to the lads to know he was safe.'

The campaign started by the men of C Company, 3rd Battalion, The Rifles, to raise money for Tangye to be found a home in the United Kingdom was successful. With the help of

Labrador Retriever Rescue Southern England and British war dog charity NOWZAD, the costs were raised and Tangye was flown to Britain, where a home was found for him.

Perhaps unsurprisingly for a country of dog lovers, Great Britain has an official means of recognising hero dogs of war: the animal equivalent of the Victoria Cross. The Dickin Medal, a bronze medallion which bears the words 'For Gallantry' and 'We Also Serve' within a laurel wreath, was named after Maria Dickin, founder of the People's Dispensary for Sick Animals (the PDSA). It was introduced to acknowledge 'outstanding acts of bravery displayed by animals serving with the armed forces or civil defence units in any theatre of war, worldwide'. It has been presented to 66 animals since its introduction in 1943.

Several Labradors have received the award for their contributions to the War on Terror, among them Sadie and Treo. Sadie, a Royal Army Veterinary Corps arms and explosive search dog and a veteran of Iraq and Bosnia, received her Dickin Medal on 6 February 2007 for an incident in 2005 when she located a remote-controlled bomb made from a pressure cooker, filled with TNT and covered with sandbags. The device, which Sadie detected through nearly a metre of concrete, was designed to kill rescue workers responding to the suicide attack. Sadie's handler, Lance Cpl Karen Yardley, shouted warnings that quickly cleared the area as a bomb disposal team moved in.

The report on the incident read:

'For outstanding gallantry and devotion to duty while assigned to the Royal Gloucestershire, Berkshire and Wiltshire Light Infantry during conflict in Afghanistan

in 2005. On 14 November 2005 military personnel serving
with NATO's International Security Assistance Force in
Kabul were involved in two separate attacks. Sadie and
Lance Corporal Yardley were deployed to search for
secondary explosive devices. Sadie gave a positive indication near a concrete blast wall and multinational
personnel were moved to a safe distance. Despite the
obvious danger Sadie and Lance Corporal Yardley
completed their search. At the site of Sadie's indication,
bomb disposal operators later made safe an explosive
device. The bomb was designed to inflict maximum
injury. Sadie's actions undoubtedly saved the lives of
many civilians and soldiers.'

Treo, also a Royal Army Veterinary Corps Arms and Explosives
Search dog, received his Dickin Medal from Princess Alexandra
at the Imperial War Museum on 24 February 2010. Treo, an
eight-year-old black Labrador, and his handler, Sergeant Dave
Heyhoe, were deployed in 2008 as part of 104 Military Working
Dogs Support Unit attached to 8 Platoon from the 1st Battalion
Royal Irish Regiment near Sangin in Afghanistan. On 15 August
2008, while acting as forward protection for 8 Platoon, Treo
located a 'daisy chain' Improvised Explosive Device which was
designed to trigger a series of bombs on a roadside where soldiers
were about to pass. It was subsequently confirmed that the device
uncovered was new to the area and would have inflicted significant casualties. Further, on 3 and 4 September 2008, Treo's actions
on patrol were reported as saving the platoon from guaranteed
casualties, again as the result of an IED. Without doubt, Treo's

actions and devotion to his duties, while in the throes of conflict, saved many lives.

Major Graham Shannon, commander of the 1st Battalion Royal Irish Regiment, said, 'Treo's nose kept my soldiers safe from the roadside bombs planted by the Taliban to maximise injuries and deaths among troops. The Military Working Dogs play a vital role in our patrols in detecting these devices and the dogs themselves show enormous amounts of courage doing this work every day, and on many occasions while under attack. It is fitting that Treo has been recognised for the protection he afforded the troops through the presentation of his award.'

In a twist to the story, it transpired that Treo had been a very naughty two-year-old who snapped and growled at people until his owners donated him to the army to 'straighten him out'. He was retired in August 2009 and adopted by his handler, Dave Heyhoe, and his family.

For those of us with a snoring dog asleep at our feet or on our bed, it may be hard to reconcile that with the image of the real 'dogs of war'. When I think of my domesticated, non-working Labrador, it's hard to imagine her serving in battle, but it is a reminder that all the virtues and attributes for which the Labrador is famed and loved worldwide, when harnessed and channelled can and have created some of the most heroic dogs of our time.

11 September 2001 was a date few of us will ever forget. Like most people, I remember the day vividly, and I remember where I was when the Twin Towers were attacked. I was filming on a wherry on the Norfolk Broads with Inca for *Countryfile*. We were sailing the calm waters of the broads, our heavy brown canvas sails propelling us along. Inca was sitting at the front of

the wherry. It was blissfully quiet, and a world away from the events that were just beginning on the other side of the Atlantic.

Alongside the 2,606 people who lost their lives when the Twin Towers collapsed was Sirius, a golden Labrador explosive detection dog who was put in his basement kennel in the South Tower when his handler, Port Authority Police Office David Lim, went to join the emergency evacuation following the initial explosion in the North Tower. When Lim set off in response to the alarm, he did not know that a plane had crashed into the top of the tower, which was then likely to collapse. Trapped in the rubble, Lim did not get out in time to go back and save Sirius. The dog died when the South Tower collapsed.

When Sirius's body was recovered, he was accorded the same respect as all the victims. All machines were silenced and everyone lined up and saluted as Officer Lim carried out his flag-draped companion while a prayer was read. Eight months later, more than a hundred dogs and their police handlers gathered in tribute to Sirius at Liberty State Park across the Hudson River. In a moving ceremony to honour the 'thousands of police dogs who play vital roles in battling terrorists, smugglers and other dangerous criminals,' officers filed by a wooden urn and a medal dedicated to Sirius. Bagpipes played and a 21-gun salute echoed. Sirius' metal bowl, recovered from the wreckage, was presented to Lim.

Two other working Labradors caught up in the blasts were awarded the Dickin Medal for their calm and dutiful heroism. Salty (also known as Dorado) and Roselle were golden Labrador guide dogs who, remarkably, led their blind owners to safety. Salty, a four-year-old, was the trusty eyes for his master, blind computer technician Omar Eduardo Rivera, who was at work on the 71st floor of the WTC North Tower. Thinking he had no chance of escape, Rivera let Salty off his lead, urging him to go, but the dog came back to him within a few minutes and nudged him towards an emergency staircase. With the help of Rivera's supervisor, Donna Enright, Salty led his master down what must have seemed an interminable spiral of 71 flights of stairs. About halfway down, a co-worker, trying to help, tried to take Salty's lead but the dog refused to leave Omar. They reached safety just before the tower collapsed.

Roselle went on to be posthumously named American Hero Dog of the Year 2011 by the American Humane Society. Roselle was her owner Michael Hingson's fifth guide dog and they had been a team for almost two years on 9/11. Roselle was asleep under the 78th-floor desk of her owner, who worked as a computer salesman, when the attack commenced. She was awoken by the plane crashing into the building 15 floors above them. Despite the smoke, panic and confusion around her, Roselle calmly led Hingson and 30 other people to stairwell B and down 1,463 steps out of the tower. The descent took just over an hour. Just after they exited the tower, the giant construction collapsed, sending up clouds of flying debris. Once clear, Roselle calmly led her owner to the safety of a subway station, where they helped a woman who had been blinded by falling debris. When they arrived home, Roselle immediately began playing with her retired guide dog predecessor, Linnie, as if nothing important had happened. When she died in 2011, Hingson wrote a book of their 9/11 experience entitled *Thunder Dog: The True Story of a Blind Man, His Guide Dog, and the Triumph of Trust at Ground Zero.*

Many Labradors were among the 300 search-and-rescue dogs that worked at Ground Zero. They worked tirelessly, often in places that were inaccessible to humans. Where even the most professional emergency service workers struggled with emotion at the scenes before them, the dogs worked diligently. Handler John Gilkey's Labrador, Bear, found remains in more than 40 sites, but he also became a focus of comfort for fellow workers. 'I remember Bear falling asleep in a firefighter's lap . . . People would stop and pet him on the pile every day. They would discuss their dogs or ones they had owned, and for a brief minute or two they had left the terror of that massacre scene,' he said. 'He helped them as much as he kept me grounded during our tour.'

Kinsey was a black Labrador whose first job after qualifying as a Canine Commando was an 11-night stint at Ground Zero. 'She wanted to find someone alive and she would bark and nip at me in frustration,' recalled Bob Deeds, her handler from Texas Task Force One. These Labradors offered the consistency of love and loyalty in a time of worldwide turmoil.

As well as the annual Dickin Medal, which has been awarded for animals showing military gallantry for over 70 years, the PDSA also awards a civilian equivalent for animal heroism, the PDSA Gold Medal. This award was instituted in 2001.

'No human or, for that matter, animal is aware of their heroic capability until placed in an extraordinary situation requiring extraordinary action. The PDSA Gold Medal recognises this.'

To date all 23 recipients awarded the PDSA Gold Medal have been dogs, two of them Labradors and both police explosives search dogs who worked bravely, obediently and tirelessly in the terror attacks in London on 7 July 2005.

Vinnie the Lab and his handler, PC Dave Coleman, were already on duty in the City when they were urgently deployed to the terrorist explosion at Russell Square tube station, during Britain's 7/7 attacks.

Vinnie began a search for secondary explosive devices to find a clear and safe route for medical assistance to reach the many casualties. Overcoming choking smoke and poor visibility, Vinnie searched the 1.6km-long route from Russell Square to the bomb-damaged train at King's Cross and completed a search of King's Cross station. Through the devastation and human trauma, Vinnie didn't hesitate in carrying out his duties. Vinnie really was one of the unsung heroes of 7/7.

Another Labrador, Billy, and his handler, PC Rob Brydon-Brown, were deployed to what they thought was a train crash at Aldgate tube station. They were met by a sea of casualties and soon realised there had been an explosion. Billy was tasked with securing the scene by searching the length of the under-ground tunnel. Despite immense heat and poor visibility, Billy didn't falter from his duties and he remained on call throughout the day, attending 21 locations in response to alerts from the public.

Another Labrador honoured as a hero in the aftermath of terrorist bombings was Zanjeer, a golden boy who worked with the bomb squad in Mumbai in March 1993 and saved thousands of lives by detecting more than 3,329 kilos of the explosive compound RDX, 600 detonators, 249 hand grenades and 6,406 rounds of live ammunition. He also helped to avert three further bomb explosions in the period after the initial blasts. Following his death at the young age of eight, from bone cancer, Zanjeer was buried with full police honours, including a wreath of flowers being laid on his body by a senior police officer.

Bosnich, a Labrador cross, was awarded a PDSA Gold Medal for bravery and gallantry in leading rescuers to 73-year-old Mark Corrie, who had gone missing on the wild Cumbrian fells in August 2006. What was remarkable was that the dog, who belonged to Corrie's daughter, Lorna Farish, was not a trained assistance dog; he was simply a family pet. His story illustrates some of the inherent instinct whereby a dog will do anything to keep the person whom he is accompanying alive and safe. Corrie and Bos had set off on their regular walk in Gelt Woods near Brampton, but the sudden onset of bad weather disorientated them. Corrie wandered around for hours, confused. In exhaustion, the elderly man took shelter in a gully on Cumrew Fell, a bleak, exposed elevation. When he failed to return home at the expected time, his daughter called the police. For two days, police search dogs and volunteers from mountain rescue teams scoured the district for man and dog, but without success. A helicopter from RAF Boulmer employing heat-seeking thermal imaging cameras also joined the search, but still there was no sign of the pair. The fortuitous rescue came when four local walkers decided to investigate a dog howling on the south side of the fell, 11 kilometres away from Brampton. At the top of the first ridge they spotted Bos, whose howl changed to a persistent bark as he engaged their attention. The dog immediately guided them to where Mark Corrie was sheltering – cold, confused, dehydrated but miraculously unhurt. It was clear the dog had used his body heat to keep the pensioner warm in between his stints of determined howling and barking. Bos stayed at the pensioner's side as they waited for the emergency services, and Mark Corrie was rescued on his 74th birthday.

The Labrador that claims the accolade of 'the most decorated dog in the world', though, is Endal, a golden-coated service dog who in his lifetime was named Dog of the Millennium, earned a PDSA Gold Medal and was the subject of a book celebrating his role in 'saving' one man and his family. Saving, in this case, was about psychological stability.

I was fortunate to meet Endal a number of times over the years. Inca, too, had the privilege to meet him. Passive and kind, Endal was the typical Lab who would sit obediently at his owner, Allan Parton's, feet.

Parton was a Royal Navy engineer who suffered a severe brain injury in a car crash in 1991 during the Gulf War. After spending five years in hospital, he returned to his wife and children a changed man. His memory had been wiped. Unable to walk, talk, read, write, or remember anyone or anything prior to the accident, Parton was confined to a wheelchair, angry, frustrated and unwilling to participate in life. During the summer of 1997, Parton's wife Sandra took her husband to a charity called Canine Partners. The charity trains dogs to help people with various impairments, enabling them to have more independence.

A young dog wandered over to his wheelchair, Parton slowly gave him a pat on the head and the dog promptly jumped on to his lap. The dog was Endal, a big bouncy Labrador who was to give Parton and his family a new lease of life. The partnership with Endal brought Parton back to emotional health. They developed an incredible bond, inventing their own sign language so that they were in cahoots together. With Endal's help, Parton could pick up anything he wanted, from a hat to a hamburger.

This incredible partnership also rekindled Parton's social skills and built his confidence and ability to talk again, because Parton had to learn to do so, if only to communicate with all the people who stopped to pat his dog. Endal notched up plenty of canine 'firsts': he was trained to withdraw cards at an ATM, empty the washing machine, bark for attention at the bar in pubs, post letters, bring over the phone and collect the knife, fork and plate for Parton's lunch.

Allan was so proud of that dog. Each time I met him, he talked of nothing but Endal. Their relationship was extraordinary. The pride Allan had for Endal was only matched by the loyalty shown by his beloved Labrador. And he wasn't just good at the soft stuff. In 2002, Endal saved Parton's life when Allan was knocked out of his wheelchair in a car park and left unconscious on the ground. Without delay, Endal put Parton in the recovery position, covered him with a blanket from the wheelchair and moved the mobile phone close to his mouth. When Parton came around, the dog trotted off to alert staff at a nearby hotel. Endal's quick actions saved him that night, just as he had saved him in so many other ways before and since.

Parton once said, 'My greatest fear, because of my head injury, is that one day when Endal is no longer faithfully by my side, because of my memory problems, I will forget him.'

It is the faithful Labrador owner's greatest fear, to forget our best friends.

CHAPTER EIGHT

YELLOW COATS

While I can't say she ever saved my life, Inca certainly helped change it in ways I could never have expected.

When I rowed the Atlantic Ocean in 2006, Marina, still then my girlfriend, packed me off with a series of envelopes. One for each day I was away. In each one was a photograph, almost all of which were of Inca, Maggi, or both. They invariably made me cry.

More importantly, they emphasised just what a perfect girl Marina was. Kind, fun, clever, thoughtful, funny, beautiful, but most importantly of all, a fellow dog lover.

Marina and I talked of little else. Our Labradors, Maggi and Inca, were like our children. I think they call them fur babies. I could never have married anyone who didn't love dogs as much as I did; my family used to joke that it would be Inca that decided the fate of various girlfriends, not me. To give them all credit, they all loved Inca, but Marina was different. Inca didn't love her, she *loved* her. What's more, Marina even had her own Lab.

We spent endless weekends exploring beaches and forests with the dogs. We travelled from Devon to Norfolk with Inca and Maggi, and at weekends we would walk the parks of London together. We were a perfect match. The four of us.

Rowing across the Atlantic gave me a chance to reflect on my life, and more importantly to plan my future. I couldn't think of anyone I'd rather spend the rest of my life with. So I made Marina a little ring made from some rope we had on our rowing boat and I proposed.

A year later, Marina and I married. We tied the knot in Portugal, too far to take our matchmakers, so instead the dogs were immortalised as figurines on top of our wedding cake, and also in a letter I read out to our guests purporting to be from the dogs, and how our marriage had in fact been entirely engineered by the dogs. It probably wasn't far from the truth.

The dogs were never far from our thoughts.

To make up for them missing the wedding, we devised our honeymoon around them. I had organised for us to spend a week on Taransay, because it was important for me to show Marina the island that had changed my life, but subconsciously I wanted to take Inca back, too, and allow her to share the experience with Maggi. By now the two dogs had become thick as thieves and were inseparable.

We loaded up the Land Rover and together, once again, we began the long overland journey up to Scotland. I'll never forget Inca's excitement when we leapt from the boat onto the shore. She was home! She raced around the island to all her favourite spots – she still knew where the fence was high enough to crawl underneath and where the gates were.

Of course, it wasn't a typical honeymoon. Goodbye tropical island, azure seas and bikinis, hello rain, mud and Gore-Tex jackets. It was cold and wet and we had to cook basic food on a woodburning stove, but it suited us. We walked and walked and walked. I introduced Marina to the island while Inca did the same with Maggi. They both had to understand how important this place was to the two of us.

When I first suggested the idea of having a dog as my luxury item for my year as a BBC castaway, I promised the filmmakers that Inca would be more than just a pet. She would be a working dog, I insisted. She would earn her keep. She would play with the children, but more importantly she would help us with the farming, rounding up pigs and sheep.

Of course, this never happened. Inca resolutely remained a pet. She was scared of the pigs and felt slightly bullied by the sheep, who would knock her sideways whenever she wandered into their field. She used to try to forage in the pigs' pen until they decided her paws looked slightly tasty. I have a hilarious photo in which it looks like Inca is being devoured by four piglets, while in fact she is just being gummed by them.

Inca was never going to work, which is surprising given how many Labradors have been used by charities and organisations to help others.

I have experienced these working dogs first hand. My father helped launch Hearing Dogs for Deaf People more than thirty years ago. The idea was simple: dogs, mainly Labradors, of course, would be trained to help those who were visually impaired. The dogs were taught to alert owners to a doorbell or a crying baby and to wake them up when the alarm bell rang and warn them if a fire or smoke alarm sounded. Above all, the dogs acted as messengers of an invisible disability. Without the bright yellow bib saying 'Hearing Dog', their owners' deafness remained invisible, often leading to conflict if someone asked them something and they didn't answer.

When Inca was seven I decided to enrol her as a Pets As Therapy dog. PAT dogs are trained to go into retirement homes and even education centres for those with learning difficulties. The idea is that a well-behaved dog goes into the home to meet all the residents because dogs bring love and calmness. To become a PAT dog, the animals need to go on a course to ensure they have the right temperament to deal with everyone from the young to the old and those with learning difficulties.

Inca had been there for so many big changes in my life. She was there through the highs and the lows. She was there for births, deaths and marriages. By my side as I lived, loved and lost, from first dates to the break-ups, through the highs of my career and the lows – the paparazzi, the tabloid tales. Inca had seen it all.

I had became dependent on Inca. She was my confidant; I told her all my fears and my troubles and she soothed and calmed me when I was anxious or stressed. A head squeeze with Inca always worked.

There are so many different ways in which people show affection to their dogs. There is, of course, the clichéd head pat. 'Pat' is a terrible description – who 'pats' their dog? To pat insinuates you bounce your hand up and down on its head. A pat is what someone unsure of a dog will do.

I prefer to stroke the head. Always moving my hand with the

fur – the hand moves from the crown of the head down onto the silky ears. I like to feel the soft velvet of the skin on the inside of the ear, feel the heat of the skin. The fur of the ear is like cashmere, fine and soft. If I'm really honest, I would often rub the ear on my cheek. Again, you stroke the nose. A Labrador loves this; not only does it help exfoliate any loose hairs on their face but they like the sensation of the touch. All Labrador owners will also be familiar with the 'Labrador nudge', where the dogs nudge their faces under your hand, compelling you to stroke them.

It has been proven by research that to stroke a dog lowers the pulse. Blood pressure can even drop. Science has proven what we dog owners have long known.

Then there is the body rub; full strokes across the back and flank of the dog. And let's not forget the belly rub – Labradors love belly rubs. Inca used to groan in ecstasy when I rubbed her belly; the sensation would often trigger a nerve that would send her leg into an uncontrollable swing.

When I was sad, I used to hold her head in my hands and hold it close to my face. Those eyes. They would heal anything. A Labrador's dark eyes have a kind of knowingness within them. Wise and worldly, they can heal a broken heart and mend a damaged ego.

Can you imagine the power of a stroke, a caress or a tummy tickle for residents in homes or people institutionalised by disabilities? Often these are people with few social interactions. In many cases they have inadvertently been starved of affection. The dog is the enabler. The dog is able to act as channel for affection and a lightning rod for stress, conducting the stress down through their paws.

Dogs often work to break down social barriers – they can often act as a trigger for conversation. Any dog owner will relate to this; you would be frowned upon if you didn't engage fellow dog walkers in idle chitchat, or in the least greet them with a cheery 'hello' or 'good morning'. It's amazing how dogs enable us to rewrite our own social rules. The dog acts as a catalyst of conversation. There is no need to talk about the weather; you can ask how old he or she is instead, or perhaps comment on their glossy coat, or ask the owner if you can say hello to them.

Inca passed all the PAT tasks with flying colours . . . until it came to the paws. The final test was the paw squeeze. You could roll Inca around on the floor and blow in her face. You could pull her tail and tweak her ears. You could scrunch her scruff and lift her gums. You could pretty much do whatever you wanted . . . except touch the paws.

Of course, all dogs have their little nuances, the little quirks that make them unique. Inca's was her paws. They were gigantic, like those of a bear, but she hated to have them squeezed. I can only attribute this to an early paw-cleaning experience from which she never fully recovered. The result of touching her paws with any pressure was that she would emit a low, deep grumble. She never snapped or bit, but she grumbled like a lion. To the uninitiated it probably sounded a little scary.

The jolly trainer had been thrilled with Inca. She had kept telling me that she was a perfect candidate for the role . . . until she squeezed her paws.

Inca emitted her low grumble. She squeezed again. Another grumble.

'Oh dear.'

It took all the persuasive distraction I could muster to take Inca's attention away from the paw squeeze for her to pass the test. It wasn't quite the calibre of her yellow-coated assistant dog cousins, but it was a start.

Inca loved her PAT visits. It was mutually beneficial, of course. Inca, like most dogs, loved physical contact. She was happiest with a hand placed upon her head or body. She would nudge you until you made contact. Even when she lay down, she would lie on top of your feet, her back wedged close to your legs.

It is the reason why Labradors have worked so well as assistance dogs, perhaps one of the oldest and most iconic being the Guide Dogs for the Blind.

There are nearly 5,000 guide dog owners in the United Kingdom, with approximately 900 new partnerships created each year, and each treasured guardian-cum-companion has an average working life of five to six years. The guide dog service is an amazing charity which receives no government funding and depends solely on public support in order to enable blind and partially sighted people to enjoy the same freedom of movement as everyone else. It costs £5 per day to support each working guide dog partnership; the lifetime cost of a dog is around £50,000.

Dogs trained to provide assistance to people with disabilities need to be confident, friendly, intelligent, willing and of a stature that makes them robust enough for a harness but small enough to curl up under the seat of a bus or train. All working dogs have to fulfil clear-cut tasks, but not even guide dogs are in total control when fulfilling their assistance role; they are in partnership with a human. Today the Labrador dominates the global guide dog population, with national breeding centres dedicated to producing dogs of suitable temperament. The Guide Dogs for the Blind Association in the United Kingdom breeds up to 1,500 puppies a year, mainly using Labradors and Golden Retrievers, as well as crosses of the two breeds.

The puppies go out to family homes for their first year then return to undertake a training programme taught by specialist instructors which typically will teach them how to lead a person in a straight line from point A to point B, unless told otherwise; to stop for all changes in elevation, such as steps and kerbs; to find doors, crossings and places which are visited regularly; to stop for overhead obstacles such as tree branches; to avoid obstacles in their path; and to resist chasing cats and squirrels. Although a trained dog will guide their owner across the road, it is up to the human to decide where and when to cross safely. The constant companionship, at home and at work, keeps up a strong and rewarding level of respect and trust between the dog and owner.

Though the Labrador was late to become the guide dog of choice (the classic working dog, the German Shepherd, was initially the most desirable canine helpmate), the history of the international guide dog movement is worth recapping as a testament to the intrinsic human drive and belief in the potential of man's relationship with the dog. The first record of a dog assisting a visually impaired person is depicted in a wall painting that was excavated at Herculaneum, preserved under 20 metres of ash following the eruption of Vesuvius in AD 79. A Chinese scroll dating from 1200, now preserved in the Metropolitan Museum in New York, also depicts a blind figure being led capably by a dog.

Similar likenesses appear in woodcuts, paintings and engravings around the world up until the eighteenth century, a time which is notable for a landmark painting by Gainsborough, *Blind Man on the Bridge*, featuring a dog showing its master the way. The question is, did these figures build on a relationship with a trusty dog they already owned and loved, or were these partnerships deliberately built up to serve a practical purpose?

The first organised attempt to use dogs as eyes came in 1780 at Les Quinze-Vingts hospital for the blind in Paris. Shortly afterwards, in 1788, Josef Reisinger, a blind sieve-maker from Vienna, trained a thick-furred Spitz so impressively that people witnessing the spectacle of dog leading man didn't believe he was blind at all. The Germans and Swiss developed their own method of training dogs, but it wasn't until the First World War, when thousands of soldiers returned from the front line having had their sight damaged by poison gas, that demand prompted a guide-dog training scheme. The catalyst was an incident seen by German physician Dr Gerhard Stalling.

Strolling through the hospital grounds with a visually impaired patient one day, he had to leave the man with his dog while he treated another urgent case. When he returned, he saw from the way the dog was behaving that it was 'looking after' the blind patient. In 1916, Dr Stalling opened the world's first guide dog school for the blind in Oldenburg. The school grew and many new branches opened across Germany – preparing up to 600 dogs a year to aid ex-servicemen and blind people in Britain, France, Spain, Italy, the United States, Canada and the Soviet Union – until a lack of suitable dogs forced closure of the venture in 1926.

Waiting in the wings – or on her Swiss farm named 'Fortunate Fields' – was an American lady, Dorothy Harrison Eustis, who took up the mantle. Having studied the successful methods for training guide dogs at a large centre in Potsdam, near Berlin – which produced 12 fully trained guide dogs a month – Dorothy and her husband George were already training German Shepherds for the army, police and customs service in Switzerland. Impressed with what the Potsdam School was achieving, she submitted an account of her visit to an American newspaper, which was published in November 1927. This resulted in a flurry of letters, including one from Morris Frank, a blind man who wanted to help introduce guide dogs to the United States, and which prompted her to try to train a dog for him to take back to the States. In April the following year, Morris Frank arrived in Switzerland and trained with guide dog 'Buddy'. When Morris and Buddy returned to New York they won over sceptical journalists by crossing a wide, busy street without injury. Lo and behold, here was America's first guide dog.

Eustis went on to launch the Seeing Eye School in America and Italy. Realising that the major problem would be training suitable instructors, she returned to Switzerland and trained four instructors; two went to the Seeing Eye School in New York, one to Italy, and one, Captain Laikhoff, came to Britain at the request of two British women, Muriel Crooke and Rosamund Bond, who had heard about the Seeing Eye. In 1931, the first four British guide dogs completed their training and the four members of that first class wrote to express gratitude for the increased mobility, dignity and independence they had thanks to their dogs:

*Not only has my dog given me glorious freedom and inde-
pendence, never known since pre-war days, but also delightful
companionship* – Allen Caldwell

*A guide dog is almost equal in many ways to giving a blind
man sight itself. Judith has been worth her weight in gold
. . . I would not be without her for a day.*

Three years later, the Guide Dogs for the Blind Association was
founded in the United Kingdom.

One of the most famous guide dogs in Britain belonged to
the blind politician, David Blunkett. Her name was Lucy the
Labrador.

Blunkett and Lucy were inseparable. Beyond his own personal
reminiscences, David Blunkett's guide dogs are immortalised in
British political history. In March 1999, as Education Secretary,
he records that he was sitting listening to a speech about education measures in the Budget given by his Conservative shadow,
David Willetts, when Lucy was sick on the carpet near the
government front bench. What to do? Deputy Speaker Michael
Lord faced the possibility of suspending the debate to allow the
vomit to be cleaned up, but Government Whip David Jamieson
stepped in, calling discreetly for cleaning materials to be brought
into the chamber and dealing with the mess himself. Meanwhile,
Lucy was led out for a bowl of water. Later in the debate, Liberal
Democrat education spokesman Dan Foster made political
mileage from the incident saying he often felt a 'sense of nausea'
when Willetts spoke. Jamieson, meanwhile, passed David
Willetts a note saying his speech had given his opposite number's

dog a turn for the worse. 'He was looking quizzical because he didn't realise what had happened, and then he roared with laughter.'

In 1994, Tony Blair, then leader of the opposition, sprang up to face John Major in Prime Minister's Questions and accidentally stood on Lucy's ear. She yowled in pain, whereupon Blair uttered an apology, words which were faithfully recorded in Hansard – marking out Lucy as surely the first dog to receive an official apology from a future prime minister.

Inca never met a prime minister, but she did once meet Michael Portillo . . .

As the years rolled on, Inca and Maggi grew older and greyer, but I was away filming in Svalbard when her world, and mine, changed forever.

We had finished filming and had returned to the main city Longbearyen, and, as with so many of my overseas shoots, I had been out of contact for nearly two weeks. In that time, Marina had left several text messages asking me to call her.

'Inca's had a funny turn,' she told me calmly when I finally got through. She explained that Inca had been asleep on her bed when she had suddenly had some sort of fit in the middle of the night. It was nearly silent, and it was only because Marina had felt her convulsing body that she knew something was wrong. She had called my father and Inca was now with him while he ran a series of tests to understand what it was and why it had happened.

If I'm honest, I wasn't really worried. I assumed it was just a one-off episode and, what's more, Marina had done a good job at playing the whole thing down. How wrong I was. I flew

home and went straight to my parents' house. I rang the doorbell and, as always, Inca came flying towards me . . . and then
she collapsed.

One of her legs was aloft and she was on her side. Her face
was contorted and she was showing her teeth in a type of grimace,
and then the shaking began. First slowly and then more violently.
Her legs kicked and white foam began to appear around her
mouth as she frothed.

I was shocked. I wanted to hold her tightly, to protect her,
but my father warned me that she might bite in her disorien-
tation. All we could do was watch helplessly.

She was having an epileptic seizure. This would be the first
of thousands as her epilepsy dominated our lives. My father
spent the next week doing every test and study he could think
of to try to discover the cause. When all that failed, he sent her
to Cambridge University where she had MRI scans of her brain
and then the rest of her body. Half her thick coat was shaved
off to allow easier access for the various tests.

In the meantime, Inca became a shell of herself. She was
permanently in some kind of drug-induced stupor. With no
proven cause, Dad had been forced to experiment with various
cocktails of drugs to try to control the increasingly common
seizures, which by this time were happening up to eight times
a day.

We had discovered that one of the best ways to pull her from
the post-trance-like stupor was with a bowl of smelly food, so
we had started stockpiling cans of wet dog food and positioned
them around the house within easy reach. For up to an hour
after each seizure, Inca would sway and stumble around the

house like a drunk. She would walk into walls and fall down stairs, and then if you held a smelly bowl of food in front of her face, she would begin sniffing at the air like she was blind. The sniffing would become more and more furious as she struggled to work out where the smell was coming from until she finally noticed the bowl in front of her face. We would then let her eat small amounts before repeating the action. I'm sure it was more to do with her deep love of food than it was scientific, but it really seemed to work.

While we were able to pull her from her post-epileptic stupor, we simply couldn't get to the root of the cause and Inca's health continued to deteriorate.

'If she gets any worse,' warned my father, 'you're going to have to make a tough decision.'

It was a thinly veiled warning that her time might be up.

I was devastated. She was only seven, and it seemed so cruel. Surely I was owed more than seven years? A dog's life already seemed too short, but this was just so unfair.

Gradually we altered the concoction of medication and with time Inca began to return to her normal self. The seizures continued, but we learned to live with them. Eventually we discovered that Inca's seizures were triggered by a sudden burst of mental and physical activity: the doorbell, pursuing a squirrel, running for her dinner, chasing a ball, or just the excitement of me coming through the door.

This meant that life became a little complicated. Both my parents and I got rid of our doorbells and placed notices warning that an 'epileptic dog' lived there and not to knock or ring the doorbell but to phone our mobiles to let us know they had arrived.

The park was much more complicated, though. A simple missed scenario of someone throwing bread to the ducks could instigate a seizure as Inca's Labrador appetite kicked in and she bolted for the bread. We always knew a seizure was about to happen because one of her hind legs would pull up uncontrollably, then her whole body would freeze and she would topple onto the ground.

While we became pretty accustomed to these daily turns, it often caught other dog walkers unawares. I lost count of the number of times I knelt at Inca's side, shouting at her to try to bring her back, when other dog walkers would run over, phone in hand ready to call the vet and offer assistance. Inevitably they thought she was dead or dying, and I always felt guilty for their concern. Not that I didn't worry myself; it was just that we dealt with the seizures so frequently that they became the norm.

It's a strange thing to say, but the epilepsy became a part of her character. Her personality. Her daily life. So much so that Marina bought her a little glittery green pencil case in which we kept her medicine. The biggest impact of her illness was that it increasingly became easier and safer to leave Inca at home when I went out or away. While I trusted Marina and my family to cope with the seizures, I was worried about leaving her with strangers, even for the shortest of times, because it was in these drunken, trance-like stupors after the seizure that Inca could spend up to an hour in an other-worldly haze. To those who didn't know her she might appear normal, but those were the times when she would get herself into trouble. Sometimes she would just bolt and run, often towards water or a road, and nothing would stop her. I would need to rugby tackle her and hold her tightly to stop her drowning or being hit by a car.

In some respects I think her epilepsy brought us even closer together. I became her full-time carer, and as such I was much more acutely aware of her behaviour. I had to second guess her instinct and read every situation.

With each seizure, Inca starved her brain of a little more oxygen, and the cumulative effect of this began to affect her behaviour. While it certainly wasn't funny, there was one incident that was as hilarious as it was heartbreaking.

We had driven out to Austria for the summer. Each year we would pack up the car and load the dogs for the long winding journey to the Austrian Alps. Once there we would spend several weeks with Marina's family high on a mountainside overlooking Salzburg. One morning I came down to breakfast.

'Have you noticed anything strange about Inca?' asked my father-in-law, Jonathan. 'She seems to be behaving a little oddly,' he continued.

I looked at Inca, who had taken her usual position in the kitchen. She was standing and wagging her tail. She looked herself.

'Inca,' I called. Her head turned and she began to move . . . backwards.

She stopped, tail wagging.

'Inca,' I called, and once again she ran backwards, away from me. Somehow, Inca had lost the ability to walk forwards. Fortunately, this quirk didn't last long, and soon enough normality returned and Inca could walk again as before.

Inca's epilepsy dominated the second half of her life. I was always on edge. I hated her seizures; they made me sad. Each one damaged her brain a little more and Dad had always warned me that one day she might not come out of one.

I'll never really know what caused the epilepsy, but it was more than likely her pedigree. The small circle of breeding in the pedigree Labrador world has led to various health issues from hips to epilepsy; you just need to look at the slightly incestuous history of the Labrador and the progenitors to realise that there has been plenty of interbreeding. I have no doubt in my mind that this was ultimately the root cause of Inca's ills. Of course, I will never really know that for a fact, but it opens the debate about where the breed has come from and, more importantly, where it is going.

The recent trend towards designer dogs, whereby two breeds are mixed together, is testament to the fact I'm not the only person worried about the health risks in pedigree dogs. By mixing two breeds, the gene pools are being further diluted, mitigating some of the health risks found in traditional breeds like the Labrador. Even when it comes to new variations of dog, the Labrador never drifts far from fashion, and while it's tempting to be swayed by one of these crossbreeds, there is still something enduring about the Labrador as we know it. It is like a classic car; however much other cars progress in terms of technology, the classics are still the most covetable. They may be temperamental and break down a great deal, they may cost a small fortune in veterinary bills, but they have stood the test of time.

I suppose in some ways, by continuing to be seduced by the pure-breed Labrador, I am part of the ongoing cause.

CHAPTER NINE

ALL THE PRESIDENTS' DOGS

There can be few things in life that are as levelling as a Labrador.

In this glorious country of ours where everything, from the clothes we wear to the accent we have, is dissected in a socio-analysis of our status, the Labrador remains relatively neutral.

It has often frustrated me how the smallest nuances of our behaviour and our choices can be used to define us by hierarchy: the place in which we live, the type of home, kitchen, car, brand of clothes we have, or the school we attended. All of these elements can be examined and used to make assumptions about our social status.

Politicians are terrified of it. Look at our current incumbent, Cameron, so worried about being classed as posh that he tries every opportunity to be the people's Prime Minister. Take his obligatory annual photo in the fish market, or at the fishmongers. He is trying to say 'look at me, supporting hard-working fisherfolk'. The fish and the market are both unclassifiable.

Even the former leader of the opposition, Ed Miliband, was at it during the General Election in May 2015. He allowed himself and his wife to be photographed posing in their annexe kitchen rather than in their large family kitchen in an effort to play down his social and financial status.

Of course, dogs have been at the forefront of political campaigns for years. The dog has given politicians the world over the chance to say something big about themselves. Indeed, the very fact that they have a four-legged furry friend speaks volumes in itself. It says, 'I am a caring, considerate person', it speaks of a selfless attitude in which you think about others more than yourself. Exactly the attributes we want from a leader.

If only Labradors could speak.

The Labrador has been the pet of choice for a number of world leaders of the modern era. Safe, loyal and biddable – there's that word again.

The Labrador is safe. It's not just their character that is safe, but also what they represent. They are apolitical. Let's take some examples. If a presidential candidate chooses a Rottweiler, a German Shepherd or a Doberman, it immediately speaks volumes about the owner. Don't get me wrong; all three have their own unique character traits, and I have met many examples of each over the years, but what do they *say* about you? They say aggressive, powerful, controlling . . .

Another example is the Bichon Frisse, the miniature Poodle or Chihuahua: again, all lovely dogs, but they say high maintenance, vain, preened. Now these might be some of the traits you are looking for in a politician, but it is also likely to divide the voters.

A politican needs a dog that defies our culture of stereotyping. Of course, the Labrador isn't without its own stereotyping. Indeed, it would be a predictable choice for our Eton-educated, Bullingdon Club fighting Prime Minister. True, they have a reputation as the country tweed choice of dog, but it is so much more complex than that. Where the stereotyped owner makes up just 2 per cent of our population, the Labrador remains our most popular dog. It doesn't add up.

The Labrador is far, far more popular than that. The Lab looks as at ease in a small terraced house as it does in a stately home. You are as likely to see one in the back of a Skoda as you are the back of a Volvo. Their popularity has not gone unnoticed by those in power, of course. Over the years Labradors have been given high status within the courts of such leaders, being accorded quasi-regal treatment, special handlers, food fit for the gods and privileged access and proximity to their masters beyond the dreams of the CIA. Not only have they been present at some of the defining moments of recent history, but they have had their own role in shaping that history. What dog owner does not talk to their dog, ask him or her rhetorical questions on a daily basis? Should I do this? Should I go ahead with that? Shall I call in the secret police? Shall I invade Ukraine?

The dogs in my life have been privy to the greatest secrets I've never told. They were there during my teenage angst. They were my loyal ears in all times of trouble or confusion.

After an official visit to Romania in the 1970s that included a hunting expedition, David Steel, the Liberal politician, found to his horror that Romanians used children instead of hunting dogs to retrieve game. Disturbed by this revelation and feeling compelled to do something about it, Steel hit upon the idea of sending his host, the Romanian leader Nicolae Ceauşescu, a Labrador puppy from a litter that Gilly, Steel's black Labrador, had given birth to. He named the puppy Gladstone 'after the Balkan connection' (referring to the then leader of the British opposition's role in denouncing the Bulgarian horrors at the time of the April Uprising of 1876, when he called up Britain to withdraw its support from the aggressor Turkey). Steel shipped Gladstone to his new Romanian master, who renamed him Corbu, meaning 'Raven'. It was an inspired gift. Dog and dictator became inseparable, and Bucharest courtiers even affixed the honorific 'Comrade' to the dog.

Wrapped in dictatorial pomp, Comrade Corbu even had his own motorcade to whisk him, nose in the air, in the back of a Dacia across Bucharest. He was later paired with Shenona, a black Labrador bitch. The two dogs ate the finest cuts of meat, spaghetti Bolognese and sausages – all of which would be first tasted and tested by a special doctor before being given to the dogs. Their coats were shampooed daily with Fa, a German brand, and sprayed with deodorant. Their paws were wiped clean with a special cloth and brush. At night, the Comrades slept on a chaise longue at the foot of the Ceauşescus' bed; by day, they lolled in their 'kennel', a villa furnished with all the bourgeois trappings of a bed, television and telephone. At 2pm, the dogs would pull a blanket over themselves with their teeth and doze until 4pm. Meanwhile, says Steel, the Romanian ambassador in London would roam Sainsbury's for dog biscuits and Winalot and would send them on a weekly basis to Bucharest by diplomatic bag.

The next occasion on which the two politicians met was at

President Tito of Yugoslavia's funeral in 1980. Ceaușescu had no recollection of Steel, and he stared blankly when the Liberal leader greeted him. A man of fine mettle and iron will, Steel pushed on with, '*Ça va, le chien?*' The penny dropped and the Romanian despot burst colourfully into congeniality and hugs.

Of course, no matter how high you elevate a dog, to 'Comrade' and even beyond, it will always remain a dog, with a dog's instincts and urges. This was shown one Sunday in 1985 when Ceaușescu paid a visit to Brâncovenesc Hospital, in Bucharest, then in danger of demolition to make way for the Boulevard of Socialist Victory. During a discussion about the future of the hospital, Corbu's attention understandably drifted off, where-upon he espied a cat. Now, the hospital had been rat-infested partly due to unaffordability of rat poison, so the doctors had resorted to using cats to cull the rodents. Corbu, by then precipitously promoted from 'Comrade' to 'Colonel', considered it his job to cull cats, and promptly ran after the feline, heedless of his master's cries to stop. When Corbu caught the cat by the throat, a bloody duel ensued. Ceaușescu screamed at his bodyguards to act. Three men leapt into the fray to prise the beasts apart. Peace was restored at the cost of three scratched bodyguards, a wounded cat and a nose-bloodied Colonel Corbu. Feeling that this was an insufficient price to pay, Ceaușescu himself then struck Corbu with his fist, more in despair than anger: his closest companion had abandoned him. For a cat.

The story didn't end there. Ceaușescu was famously paranoid about disease and infection, and, fearing poison, he never wore the same clothes twice. So he ordered for the Securitate to have the cat checked for disease. The hospital was turned upside down as doctors and nurses sought out cats and produced them for inspection by the Securitate to find the one that had earlier caused the ruckus. It wasn't until 10.30 that night that the culprit, one of many cats caught that evening, was identified by a bloody gash to his side. It was immediately hustled into a secure guarded room while the hospital's carpenter fashioned a special cage for the feline. The following morning the cat was taken to the Institute of Veterinary Medicine to be checked for disease. After a fortnight, the cat got the all clear. During those two harrowing weeks, Colonel Corbu was banned from Ceauşescu's presence. Nevertheless, the doctors knew that the incident had sealed the hospital's fate. It is ironic that a man as paranoid about health as Ceauşescus should preside over the closure of a hospital, more so because of a fight between a cat and a 'Colonel'. But at least Corbu had proven his credentials as a hunting dog.

Vladimir Putin is quickly becoming the bogeyman of our age. His muscle-flexing rhetoric is bringing Europe to the brink of war, but apart from his warmongering, little is known about the man who many describe as the most powerful in the world.

While few Russians know much about Vladimir Putin's family, almost all Russians and many others beyond Russia's borders know about Koni. As H. Goscilo writes, Koni 'serves as Putin's attribute not only in children's pictures of him, where Koni is depicted as Putin's sidekick, but also elsewhere, and with more obvious importance than the human members of Putin's family. Koni definitely holds an important place in the public's imagination as a metonym of Putin's power.'

Born in a government cynology centre in Noginsk, a few kilometres east of Moscow, which specialises in breeding crack dogs for search and rescue, Koni is a female black Labrador Retriever which was given to Putin in 2000 by Sergey Shoygu, General of the Army and Minister of Emergency Situations. Putin uses his beloved Labrador Koni for his own political power in the games of diplomatic one-upmanship that are part of the cut and thrust of life in Russia. Indeed, a cold war of sorts is being waged between Russia and the West in which presidential pets are the weapons. As George W. Bush recalls in his memoir, *Decision Points*, while he and Putin strolled the birch-lined grounds of Putin's dacha one summer, a large black Labrador bounded up to them. Putin turned to Dubya and said, 'You see? Bigger, stronger and faster than Barney [Dubya's Scottish terrier].'

In a society like Russia, which favours strong leaders and where expressions of certain emotions can be interpreted as a weakness, Koni offers an emotional crutch. As Putin once said at a press conference in response to a question about his moodiness, 'As far as bad moods go, of course I have them like any other person, but in those cases I try to consult with my dog Koni – she gives me good advice.'

Koni has become elevated to something of a national icon. She accompanies the Russian president to meetings and to greet world leaders. When Putin first met Angela Merkel, he brought Koni, knowing that the Germany Chancellor is afraid of dogs, having been bitten by one as a child. In December 2003, when Koni gave birth to eight puppies, which were given away to Russian citizens, politicians and foreign ambassadors, Koni was hailed as 'a Mother Hero', the official title that the Soviet State, keen to raise the national birth rate, bestowed on unusually fertile women. In February 2005, there was even a youth campaign to promote Koni to President.

For Putin personally, Koni seems to be the wife figure that perhaps he otherwise lacks. At a press conference in Sochi in 2003, the officially sponsored newspaper *Rossiyskaya Gazeta* reported that when it was time to begin the meeting, Putin's security detail tried to prevent Koni from entering the meeting room. Koni was having none of it. Pushing her way past the guards, she rushed down a staircase to confront Putin as he and a group of journalists made their way to the room. Turning to face Putin, Koni barked loudly at the President, as if to say, 'Where the hell do you think you're going without me?' Among journalists present was Irena Lesnevsky, founder and owner of REN TV, one of the largest private television channels in Russia. 'So who else here can bark at the President?' she demanded.

Koni repeated the trick one year later when, at a children's New Year party at the State Kremlin Palace, she gave security guards the slip and managed to join Putin on stage while he was in mid-speech to media, politicians and the public.

Food is, of course, the Achilles heel of powerful leaders, no more so than in Russia, which has a tradition of Czaricide by poison. It is known that Vladimir Putin has all his food tested for toxins, and so, not surprisingly, Koni's eating habits are food for debate and speculation. Does the same presidential protection extend to her? Putin once issued a press statement saying, 'Please don't feed my dog.' Koni, however, has her own ideas on the matter. At a meeting of members of the United Russia Party at Putin's residence at Novo-Ogaryovo, convened to discuss the local food industry, a special tea was prepared to bring the meeting to a close. While the meeting was still in session, Koni rocked up and wolfed all the food, pastries, biscuits and jellied puddings. As an astonished bodyguard said, 'Koni ate everything!'

These incidents raise questions about the effectiveness of Putin's close protection bodyguards. After all, if a dog can elude them . . . ? Putin's first question upon attending a 2008 demonstration of the Global Navigation Satellite System (GLONASS) that the Russian army had developed in answer to the American GPS system, was, 'Can I use it on my dog?' Later that year, Koni was fitted with the first GLONASS-enabled collar. Should any of Putin's rivals or enemies wish to bug or otherwise harm Koni, they must somehow distract the attention of 21 geostationary satellites that track Koni's exact whereabouts 24/7.

Doubtless, Koni is indeed bigger, tougher, stronger, faster and meaner than Barney, Dubya's terrier. It also appears that she is tougher, smarter, faster and meaner than Putin's bodyguards, too. Koni for President!

The United States also has a rich tradition of presidential dogs. Indeed, the announcement of the First Dog is arguably as important as the President himself.

'You want a friend in Washington?' Harry S. Truman, US president (1945–53), famously said. 'Get a dog.' Truman himself shunned canine company (in 1947, he passed on a gifted blond Cocker Spaniel by the name of Feller) and indeed he preferred to hustle pet-free. However, other US presidents from George Washington onwards have kept a colourful menagerie of pets – from horses, goats and parrots to lions, hyenas and even alligators. (John Quincy Adams' donated alligator terrorised White House guests from its bathroom nest; President Hoover's son Henry kept a pair that sometimes roamed the White House grounds.)

Having served his first term of office dog-free, Clinton decided one year into his second term to get a dog. Bill, Hillary and Chelsea Clinton studied various breeds. 'Chelsea wanted a teeny-weeny dog she could carry around with her, and Bill wanted a big dog he could run with,' wrote Hillary in *Living History*. 'We worked through that and finally decided that a Labrador would be just the right size and temperament for our family and the White House.'

So, in December 1997, a three-month-old chocolate Labrador puppy was acquired from Tony Harrington, a lawyer from Washington DC, who bred dogs. When puppy met president and the canine scampered into Clinton's arms, both parties were smitten. 'All we had to do was figure out a name,' continues Hillary. 'Buddy' evoked Bill Clinton's great-uncle Henry 'Buddy' Grisham, who had recently died and whom Clinton often described as a major influence.

Before naming their puppy, though, the Clintons consulted one of the White House butlers, name of Buddy Carter, to see if he objected to their puppy sharing his name. Carter loved the idea, and began to identify with the dog. Months later, when Buddy the dog was sent for neutering, Buddy the butler was seen shaking his head and muttering, 'Not a good day for Buddy today. Not a good day at all.'

Bill and Buddy the Labrador quickly became firm friends. Evoking Truman, Clinton's spokesman Mike McCurry said, 'It is the President's desire to have one loyal friend in Washington.' Buddy appears to be the first and so far only example of a Labrador as First Canine.

'We brought our family traditions, favourite pictures, and

personal mementos to make the White House feel more comfortable,' wrote Hillary Clinton when the Clintons moved into the White House. 'But it wasn't until . . . Buddy walked in with his rawhide bone that this house became a home. Pets have a way of doing that.'

Buddy the dog fell in with Bill Clinton's routine. He slept at his feet in the Oval Office and stayed up late. He strolled the White House grounds with Bill, and accompanied him to Camp David. He was present at the historic Israeli–Palestine peace talks in 1998 that took place between Netanyahu and Arafat, and he even adopted some of his master's characteristics. 'He loved people, possessed a sunny optimistic disposition, and had the ability to focus and concentrate with singular intensity,' wrote Hillary. When the Lewinsky scandal broke and Bill was in the doghouse, Buddy alone kept him company. Buddy's two obsessions were tennis balls and food; he would chase and retrieve balls until he dropped, 'then he'd get up and look for his dinner.'

While family life centred on Buddy, Socks, the feisty adopted stray cat, felt usurped. Buddy and Socks' long-standing feud became infamous, so much so that it was eventually decided that one of them must go: Socks was given away to Clinton's former personal secretary, Betty Currie.

Like Socks, Buddy littered a family of fan clubs and websites in his honour. In her book, *Dear Socks, Dear Buddy: Kids' Letters to the First Pets*, Hillary Clinton explained how letters to Buddy and Socks were sorted, read and answered at the US Soldiers' and Airmen's Home.

After President Clinton's second term expired and the family moved to their home near Chappaqua, NY, Buddy became a familiar sight tugging on his leash or chasing tennis balls. Tragically, Buddy's sunny exuberance eclipsed him. On 2 January 2002, while playfully hounding a contractor's van into the street outside the Clintons' home, to the despair of chasing Secret Service agents, he died when a car struck him. Buddy was rushed to Chappaqua Animal Hospital where he was pronounced dead. The Clintons were away on holiday.

'We are deeply saddened by Buddy's death,' said the Clintons in a statement. 'He was a loyal companion and brought us much joy. He will truly be missed.'

In 2005, the Clintons adopted Seamus, their second chocolate Labrador.

Another American statesman, Henry Kissinger, was a Labrador lover. In 1988, Kissinger lost his yellow Labrador Tyler to cancer. He was heartbroken and the situation brought out the softest side of the formidably tough National Security Advisor who had served under Presidents Richard Nixon and Gerald Ford. Gregory MacEwen, who treated the dog, was impressed that Kissinger got right down on his knees in his three-piece silk suit while Tyler lay prone and whispered into his dog's ear how much he loved him. When Kissinger was Secretary of State, he sometimes brought his Labrador to the office. Mighty are some of the names today of important US diplomats who, as assistants to Mr Kissinger, were awarded the dubious honour of taking his Lab for a walk around the block. One neighbour of Kissinger in New York recalls watching Kissinger take his ailing black Labrador out for walks in an 'open red children's wagon'. The Kissingers later had a black Labrador named Abigail. In 1994,

Kissinger successfully lobbied to have a Labrador Retriever reprieved from death by lethal injection for chasing postmen: Smokey, a five-year-old Labrador Retriever from Danville, Virginia, was found guilty of chasing (but not biting) three mail carriers in his Danville neighbourhood, thus becoming the first dog to face sentencing under Danville's tough 'three mail carriers and you're out' ordinance. Smokey was sentenced to die by lethal injection, but the case turned political when 40 members of the Italian Senate signed a petition on Smokey's behalf, and that world-class humanitarian and retriever owner Henry Kissinger urged the judge to 'Restore the dog to the owner and tell the mailman to take a different route.'

Dick Cheney, Vice President of the United States from 2001 to 2009 under George W. Bush, owned two Labradors; Jackson (black) and Dave (golden). In 2011, Dave hit the headlines for all the wrong reasons. After launching an attack on Barney, Dubya's feisty Scottish terrier (the one whom Vladimir Putin liked to mock), in full view of other guests, he was banned from the main lodge at Camp David. Dave would regularly accompany Cheney to the US presidential retreat in Maryland, and on this occasion, he joined his master in the Laurel Lodge, scene of official meals and meetings. 'No sooner had we walked inside did Dave catch sight of the president's dog, Barney,' relates Cheney in his memoir, *In My Time*. 'Hot pursuit' ensued. Clearly, Dave subscribed to his master's zero tolerance to terrorism and launched a pre-emptive strike to neutralise the terrier. The dogs ended up duelling in the dining room, where wives of several Cabinet members were enjoying breakfast.

'What's going on here?' demanded Dubya on seeing the

mayhem. It was not an unreasonable question. Cheney sedated Dave with a pastry from the breakfast buffet and then hauled the mutt back to the cabin where he and his wife Lynne were staying.

'I hadn't been there long when there was a knock at the door,' Mr Cheney writes. 'It was the camp commander. 'Mr Vice President,' he said. 'Your dog has been banned from Laurel.'

In Dave's defence, there is ample video evidence of Barney's aggressive tendencies (possibly an insecure reaction to jibes from Vladimir Putin). In 2008, Barney bit a Reuters' reporter on camera, causing a wound that had to be patched up by the White House physician.

Ever since Napoleon Bonaparte's life was saved by a Newfoundland, when the non-swimming French leader slipped and fell from a ship into the sea, dogs and French Heads of State have had a close bond, possibly closer than between French Heads of State and other human beings. 'Here, Gentlemen,' said Bonaparte, upon safely reaching shore on the back of the Newfoundland, 'a dog teaches us a lesson in humanity.' In the same vein, De Gaulle once said, apparently paraphrasing Harry S. Truman, 'The better I get to know men, the more I find myself loving dogs.'

Just as dogs have historically accompanied the French nobility, so in recent years they have become power accessories to the country's democratically elected politicians. Labradors in particular seem to be the preferred breed. This might seem a strange choice; Labradors are an unlikely pet for a French president. Few of the characteristics commonly associated with Labradors seem particularly, well, French: loyal, obedient,

playful, happy, gregarious, charmingly naïve, bourgeois, reassuring and trustworthy. Yet every French president since the
early 1970s has owned at least one Labrador.

While in power, Valéry Giscard d'Estaing had two black
Labradors: Jugurtha, a chocolate male, and Sandringham Samba,
a black male that HM the Queen gave d'Estaing in 1976 (Samba
was trained in the Queen's English, suggesting a cunning ruse
to introduce the language of Shakespeare and Churchill into the
highest political circles of France). In retirement d'Estaing
acquired two more Labradors: Beauly and Typhon. '*Il poursuit:
'Ce sont des chiens très accueillants. Quand je reviens, ils sautent
en l'air de joie. Je n'ai jamais rencontré d'être humain qui, lorsque
je reviens, saute avec une telle allégresse'.* 'They are very friendly
dogs,' he said. 'When I come back, they jump in the air with
joy. I've never met a human being who, when I get back, jumps
with such joy . . .' Today, ex-President d'Estaing owns Spinee,
an 'adored' golden Labrador Retriever who, in 2014, underwent
surgery, much to the consternation of both the former president
and Spinee's army of fans.

Labradors were the preferred power pooch for François
Mitterrand, Jacques Chirac and Nicolas Sarkozy, who named
them Baltique (black female), Maskou (black male) and Clara
(sand-coloured female) respectively. Mitterrand, a serial
Labradiste, also had Nile, a black male. Attitudes towards dogs
became a political hot *pomme de terre* when, during the 1988
presidential election campaign, Jacques Chirac tore snarling into
François Mitterrand, accusing him of raising the tax on dog food.

Baltique, Mitterrand's Labrador, had the run of the Élysée
Palace. According to Daniel Gamba, author of *Interlocuteur*

privilégié, j'ai protégé Mitterrand, when he went missing, life at
the Palace stopped dead. At Mitterrand's funeral in January
1996, he had made arrangements for Baltique to travel alongside
his coffin in the State cortège as it wound from Paris to
Mitterrand's final resting place at Jarnac.

When Jacques Chirac finally won power in 1995, his Labrador
Maskou was wrongly accused of devouring the Élysée Palace
ducks. However, rumours persist of canine misdemeanour during
Sarkozy's rule. The Élysée's famous Salon d'Argent is almost
unchanged from the sumptuous room that Napoleon's sister
Caroline Murat created in 1807, where Napoleon signed his abdi-
cation in 1815 and where President Félix Faure died in the arms
of his mistress, Marguerite Steinheil, in 1899. But those fang marks
in the chair legs, and those stains on the soft furnishings – whose
are those? Sarko's incontinent alpha pooches, Toumi the
Chihuahua, Clara the Labrador and Dumbledore the Terrier, were
allegedly partial to gilded silk-swathed nineteenth-century furniture: as an hors d'oeuvres they snacked on antique sofa legs, as
an entrée they gnawed at braided chaises longues, and for dessert
they sunk their teeth into silk cushions. The repair bill ran to
thousands of euros, excluding the cost of the new braids, silk
covers and the time of the Mobilier National staff. If Sarko
couldn't control his dogs, how, one might ask, could he control
France? More importantly, this canine affront was a logical but
dramatic response to the threat of a tax on dog food: a tax on
dog food is a tax on France's patrimony!

In Britain, Labradors have proved useful both as PR
tools and as voter bait to politicians on either side of the
political divide.

On the left, the Jarrow March of 1936 got a PR boost when Paddy, a black Labrador, joined in and was adopted as the march's official mascot and even appeared on the cover of the newspapers. Harold Wilson, two times Prime Minister, used his golden Labrador, also called Paddy, not only to burnish his image while being photographed on holiday in the Isles of Scilly, but also to cover up his own stupidity: in August 1973, Wilson, yet to serve his second term at Number 10, fell from a dinghy into the sea and nearly drowned. Jo Haines, the Labour leader's spin doctor, blamed Paddy for the accident, despite Isabel Wolff, whose family rescued the weasel Wilson, insisting that she saw Paddy chained to a hut on the beach, looking 'affable and unperturbed'. Clearly, Paddy voted Conservative. Ken Livingstone, ex-MP and ex-Mayor of London, campaigned for the mayoralty in 2012 alongside Coco, his golden Labrador. Livingstone lost in the poll to Boris Johnson.

On the right, David Burrowes, MP (Conservative) for Enfield, Southgate, uses Cholmeley his golden Labrador to help raise awareness of responsible dog ownership. Neil Parish, MP (Conservative) for Tiverton and Honiton, owns Wilberforce, a golden Labrador and winner of Westminster Dog of the Year 2012. Edwina Currie, ex-MP for South Derbyshire, says that George, her chocolate Labrador, is 'Here for me when people are horrid,' adding superfluously that George is as 'daft as a brush'.

While dogs have obvious photogenic appeal, Andrew Murrison, MP (Conservative) for South West Wiltshire, put his finger on another reason why democratically elected politicians prefer pooches. Buster, his black Labrador, is an 'asset' on the doorsteps, he told the *Daily Mail,* because, 'Constituents' dogs can normally smell Buster on my clothes, and this makes them very friendly to me.' Result: Murrison's 'animal magnetism' wins votes.

I love the idea that this simple, humble, honest dog has been on the front line of the political elite for decades, if not centuries. It always surprises me that David Cameron doesn't have a Labrador; it would be the perfect dog for a country-living, family-loving prime minister. Come to think of it, he doesn't have a dog. Maybe that's the reason why no one really likes him. As I say, never trust a man who doesn't like dogs.

From dictators to presidents, meglomaniacs to prime ministers, all have shared their lives with the humble Labrador. Throughout history these dogs have been privy to conversations and decision making that have affected us all. If only Labradors could speak.

CHAPTER TEN

LAB OF ALL TRADES

I never cease to be amazed at the ingenuity and enterprise shown by Labradors when they are trained and willing to take on human tasks that increase the quality of life of others, particularly individuals with physical disabilities. They are often best friend, nurse, personal assistant and au pair (or should that be au paw), complete with wagging tail.

The list of roles we have found for Labradors keeps on growing. One of the new areas for these dogs has been to help children with autism. Eleven-year-old Charlie McGowan was three when he was diagnosed with autism. An apparently healthy little toddler, he lost all linguistic ability at the age of two. He wouldn't allow anyone to touch him and he stopped making eye contact with people, including his mother, Kirsty. He would only sleep for one hour each night, meaning that he was awake for the remaining 23 hours of the day. Charlie would become extremely stressed and repeatedly banged his head until he bled. His autism was so severe that his mother was warned that by the time he turned 10 she wouldn't be able to look after him herself. Kirsty didn't give up, though. Determined to ensure she had tried everything to help her son, she realised she would have to do something radical. Although Charlie could cope in his own home with a support system around him, leaving the house was almost impossible for him. 'We couldn't attend doctors' appointments or even go into the shops,' said Kirsty. 'In a supermarket Charlie would become so distressed that he would drop to the floor, scream, and bang his head repeatedly. The only way I could get Charlie out of the house was in a wheelchair. However, if a plane went overhead or if a bus stopped close by, Charlie would become stressed and inconsolable. We were unable to get out more than once a week, it was just too much of a challenge.'

Support Dogs was set up to increase the independence and quality of life for people with medical conditions. The charity provides, trains and supports specialist assistance dogs to provide help with everyday tasks for people with physical disabilities, give advance warning of seizures for people with epilepsy, and provide safety and support for children with autism and their families. Kirsty put her son's name on the waiting list. 'It was the best thing I could have ever done. I spent five years hoping and praying every day that we would get the call. Then finally it came and it changed our lives. There was a dog for Charlie, a black Labrador named Bailey. Charlie's autism is so severe I was unsure how much difference Bailey could make, but I couldn't have been more blown away.' Charlie had never walked on his own two feet since he was two and a half years old. When he was first attached to Bailey, he walked straight down the street for the first time. 'After seven and a half years my son was walking on his own,' his mother recalls. 'It makes me want to cry every time I think about it. Now we have Bailey, we finally have a life. When we leave our front door Bailey is a godsend and Charlie's best friend. Once he's attached to Bailey the world makes sense. Just having him attached to him means he can process sensory information better. And if something worries Charlie, he bends down and hugs Bailey. It's not just Charlie's life that Bailey has changed. He knows when I'm becoming stressed or anxious and calms me down. I love him and I'm so grateful for everything he does for us both.'

Support Dogs is also responsible for training the remarkable Hetty, a Labrador cross who won a Guardian Angel Award in the augural Britain's Animals Honours Award Show, broadcast on ITV in April 2013. Hetty is thought to be the world's first guide dog who is also a trained medical assistance dog. Officially she is classified as a Dual Assistance guide dog. Specifically, she can detect the signs of a seizure before her owner, Tony Brown-Griffin, who is registered blind and has intractable epilepsy, suffers one by recognising the physiological changes which are invisible to the human eye. In the past, Tony's epileptic fits had caused her to smash headfirst through a glass shower screen, fracture her wrists and break ribs falling in the street. 'The unpredictability of seizures is frightening – not knowing if it's going to happen in the middle of a busy road,' says Tony. 'Even going up the stairs would be terrifying because if I had a seizure I could fall. So much of what I do revolves around Hetty. She is fundamental to what I do. Everything I can do is because of her. Without her, I'd be stuck.'

The clever thing is that Hetty gives different signals to

distinguish the severity of the oncoming attack. Sensing a minor seizure, Hetty nudges Tony and rests her head on her lap, giving her 15 minutes to prepare herself to sit somewhere soft until it passes. If it's a major or life-threatening seizure, she paws Tony's leg and Tony knows she has precisely 42 minutes to prepare. Hetty will also lie with Tony as a comfort until she recovers. A fit can last between five and ten minutes and Tony suffers approximately two major and four minor attacks a week. Hetty is also vigilant to ensure that Tony's two young children don't witness their mother in the hold of these scary fits. Tony lost her sight six years ago, so Hetty also does the jobs that a traditional guide dog undertakes – helping Tony dress by removing her socks and trousers and helping with sleeves, taking the laundry out of the washing machine, even stripping the household beds.

As well as acting as a guide and seizure dog, Hetty has also picked up new skills. Tony also has severe food allergies, and when she was new to her, Hetty would try to alert her to a reaction but Tony would ignore her and tell her to lie down as she wasn't acting as if it were a seizure alert. 'Then one day my brother-in-law said, "Should Hetty be standing on the table?" and I turned around and she was there. Again I told her off, but about 10 minutes later I started feeling really bad with an anaphylatic shock reaction. We realised that was what she was trying to warn me of. Now she jumps up at my belt to let me know. People assume that she's misbehaving – they misinterpret her. Or when we're out, people assume she's got a sore paw because she holds it up slightly. When I explain what she does, they're always impressed.'

What other good uses can a dog's extraordinary instinct and vigorous sense of smell be put to? Dr Claire Guest, a psychologist, was convinced that dogs could sniff out cancer. While she was working to prove her hunch, she received the most emotive affirmation that she was right about the potential of dogs to operate as medical detection agents.

In the middle of experiments to train her own Labrador, Daisy, to pick up the smell of chemicals given off by tumour cells, Daisy began to act strangely around her. Instead of being her normal, placid self, Daisy seemed uptight and uncharacteristically attentive – exactly the kind of behaviour that she had been taught to display if she detected the odour of cancer. Had the dog's work/life balance gone awry? No. Dr Guest could never have anticipated that the first person Daisy would diagnose would be herself.

'She kept jumping up on me,' she told the *Telegraph*. 'One day she bumped into my chest with her nose. It was unusually sore, and there seemed to be a lump there. I had a fine needle biopsy, but it came back clear.'

After more unsettling behaviour from Daisy, Dr Guest had a core needle biopsy and was diagnosed with early stage breast cancer. She underwent treatment and has since been given the all clear.

'Had I not had Daisy's early warning, I would have had a very poor prognosis,' she said. 'It would have gone undetected for much longer and could have been more serious. I have my dog to thank for the fact that I'm standing here today.'

That was in 2009, when Daisy was just a puppy, and the charity working on this controversial technique was only one year old.

Dr Guest's dog is now the Medical Detection Dogs organisation's most distinguished 'advanced cancer dog', able to detect different cancers through smelling a patient's breath, urine or skin. She heads up a growing number of dogs now being trained as 'pattern recognition biosensors' to detect cancer in this way and, as the pioneer, was awarded the Blue Cross Medal for her work. The medal is awarded by the Blue Cross charity to an animal that has changed or saved someone's life – and Daisy had (to date then) sniffed more than 6,500 samples and detected more than 550 cases of cancer.

Daisy now helps to train a team of 12 dogs at the Medical Detection Dogs' head office and is a senior consultant for the United Kingdom's first ever trial using canines to detect breast cancer.

The science behind it is simple in theory: to harness a dog's acute sense of smell to pick out chemicals given off in cancer cells in samples of a patient's breath, skin or urine. The dogs do not meet the patients who have provided samples: they work in a laboratory setting, sniffing along a row of samples attached to a small conveyor belt. On the command of 'Seek-seek', they sniff all the samples and return to sit and bark by any which emit a cancerous smell.

The idea of your pet dog having a sixth sense and trying to warn you about something is not uncommon, but it was two doctors, Hywel Williams and Andres Pembroke, who first put forward the idea of dogs as potential medical detective agents in a 1989 article in *The Lancet*. Their claims were re-aired on BBC Radio 4 in 2001 by the orthopaedic surgeon Dr John Church (who had equally controversially introduced wound-cleaning maggots to the NHS). Dr Guest heard the programme, contacted Dr Church and together they formed a research team at the Buckingham NHS Trust, with funding from an anonymous philanthropist. They conducted ever-larger clinically robust, proof-of-principle studies – largely detecting for cancer of the bladder, breast and prostate – and published the encouraging results in the *British Medical Journal.* The voice of the sceptics has now reduced to a whisper and several cancer specialists have come out in support of the scheme. For example, Dr Alan Makepeace, a senior oncologist at the Mount Vernon Cancer Centre in Middlesex, who was initially dismissive of the involvement of dogs, told the *Telegraph*: 'The data is robust. Dr Guest's passion is driven by good science, not anecdotal evidence. There is so much we don't know about the natural world. A more effective early test could be worth its weight in gold.'

The results are not 100 per cent accurate, but the charity's recent study into the detection of prostate cancer shows the dogs achieved 93 per cent reliability compared with the 75 per cent detection of patients who don't actually have cancer when examined after traditional PSA tests, a blood test which can detect early stage prostate cancer. This work is being developed to examine the potential of offering second-line screening for men.

It would be impractical to use dogs pervasively, but their value could lie in determining whether further invasive and uncomfortable tests are needed when a patient is presenting inconclusive symptoms. Already, a prototype 'electronic dog nose' has been developed by an Israeli-Arab chemical engineer at the Laboratories of Nanomaterial-based Devices in Haifa.

Hossam Haick has created the 'NANOSE', which it is hoped could be used to analyse a patient's breath for traces of cancer.

As the pioneering charity in this area, Medical Detection Dogs has two aims in its cancer work. First, to assist scientists like Hossam Haick through their research into the development of electronic systems (E noses) in order to facilitate the early detection of cancer through cheap non-invasive tests. Second, in the short term, the charity's team of cancer dogs can provide second-line screening for cancers that are very difficult to diagnose reliably, such as prostate cancer. Dr Guest acknowledges the limitations of introducing dogs to the NHS. 'It would be impossible to have a trainer and specialist dog in every surgery,' she said. 'But dogs can be used behind the scenes to screen samples. Dogs enjoy it. There's no reason why they can't screen large numbers of samples if they get a biscuit at the end.'

The Medical Detection Dogs Centre also trains canines for purposes other than cancer detection. People with nut allergies can apply for a dog trained to detect nut traces in their immediate environment. Those with severe type one diabetes can receive a dog that will alert them when their blood sugar is reaching dangerous levels. A similar service can be provided to sufferers of Addison's disease, a hormonal disease that causes the adrenal glands to malfunction and not produce enough of the steroid hormone known as cortisol.

Karen – one of many to consider themselves blessed in being supported by Medical Detection Dogs – refers to her chocolate Labrador Coco as her 'knight in shining armour with a waggy tail'. Karen suffers from Addison's disease and her condition was exacerbated due to the removal of tumours found on her adrenal glands, which left her with no cortisol reserve in her body at all. If cortisol levels become dangerously low, the patient's condition becomes critical and can lead to death if they are not treated quickly. An Addisonian crisis causes severe pain, convulsions and unconsciousness; pain seizures which lead to collapse and hospitalisation; severe allergic responses, and narco-lepsy – a malfunction of the sleep/wake regulating system which causes sleep attacks and paralysis.

Coco is the first dog in the world that has been trained to assist an Addison's disease sufferer. Karen has very little time from the moment of starting to feel unwell to a full-blown crisis, but Coco, who carries her injection kit with him in his vest, will warn her when the cortisol levels are dropping and will persist until he gets the message through. 'People have already noticed that I am much more confident since having Coco,' says Karen. 'I sleep better knowing he will alert me if my levels drop while I'm asleep. I can also relax when out and about knowing that Coco is there to look after me. As long as I have my knight in shining armour with a waggy tail with me by my side, I'm not scared of anything anymore.'

Diabetes is on the rise in Britain and thus the avoidance of dangerously low blood sugar levels (hypoglycaemia) is an acute daily issue for many people. When the condition is accompanied by loss of warnings it has a dramatic effect on the lives of both the person with diabetes and their family because low blood sugar levels are very dangerous if left untreated. Symptoms vary from confusion to seizures to comas, and can become life-threatening. An inability to detect a 'hypo' is particularly common in young children and adolescents as a result of their stage of growth and development. With their amazing sense of smell the dogs are trained to detect minute changes in blood sugar levels. When these levels fall or rise outside the normal range they will warn their owner, get help and fetch any vital medical supplies.

In the case of Cherry and Zeta, a characterful black Labrador who was Britain's first Diabetic Hypo-alert dog, it has been a joint learning curve. Zeta was deemed the family pet after being declared not fit enough to train as a guide dog, but when Cherry, who had been an insulin-dependent diabetic since he was 29, began to lose his hypoglycaemic warning symptoms, his wife enquired about re-training Zeta as one of the Diabetic Alert Dogs she knew existed in Australia and North America. She contacted Claire Guest, who came to stay for a few days and taught her how to train Zeta to alert when Cherry's blood sugar was low. Zeta was a quick learner and gave Cherry and his wife a new sense of security. Like all Labradors, though, she has her own personality quirks. In Zeta's case, she doesn't do night duty! She sleeps and snores through everything.

The Labrador's finely honed skill to detect scents also comes in very useful for the police force. Just as they are an integral part of bomb detection teams in the army, Labradors are an important element in the detection of drugs as well as missing persons and police suspects.

A law enforcer also enjoys extra personal security with a dog. In the fifteenth century, parish constables often took their dogs to work for company and what would now be termed 'back-up'. According to the Metropolitan Police Service (MPS), the first use of dogs by the police was believed to be in 1888 when two bloodhounds were used during the Jack the Ripper murders to try to track the killer through the streets of Whitechapel and Spitalfields. The Home Office had suggested Sir Charles Warrens, Head of the MPS during the Ripper investigation, use bloodhounds to sniff out the murderer. Warren himself was sceptical about a dog's ability to pick up one scent from pavements where people had been walking all night, but, after trials in two London parks, he was won over and gave instructions that, in the event of another murder, the victim's body must not be touched until bloodhounds could be brought to it and put on the scent. The policy was short-lived, though, because the owner of the bloodhounds couldn't agree on a suitable fee for the services of their dogs with the police. On the sole occasion they were called upon in the immediate aftermath of the murder of Mary Kelly, the owner had taken back their dogs so that they were no longer available to the police.

In 1914, following experiments in Germany and elsewhere in Europe, the Met introduced 172 dogs of various breeds to accompany officers on patrol. In that inaugural year of police dog use, an officer and dog were commended for saving a person from drowning in a lake. The dog was rewarded with a new collar.

1938 was the Year of the Police Labrador. Two Labradors became the first genuine police dogs and their beat to patrol was in Peckham, South London. Following the Second World War, six Labradors were reintroduced to combat crime, supplemented in 1948 by the first German Shepherd to be employed by the police. The dogs were very successful and their numbers grew to 90 by 1950 within the dog section, which was then based at Imber Court, in Surrey. In 1954 the current MPS Dog Training establishment at Keston, in Kent, was opened, where all dog-training courses now take place. Since then the Dog Support Unit has been at the forefront of police dog training, constantly exploring new ways to use the special abilities of these animals to improve officer and public safety, and to detect and prevent crime. Today, around 250 dogs of various types work across the MPS.

The role of the Dog Support Unit (DSU) is to provide police dog and handler teams to support their colleagues across London, and to respond to emergency calls where their unique skills can be used to help make London safer. Specific dogs have specific skills. For example, German and Belgian Shepherd dogs most often act as general-purpose dogs to undertake roles such as – and here is the official job description – searching for suspects and missing people, locating objects dropped or concealed during a criminal incident, following a track left by a person on the ground, chasing and detaining a person who runs away when challenged to stop, disarming violent armed suspects and controlling hostile crowds.

Some of the more specialist skills include support of firearms teams and something called – with tremendous understatement – 'line access' work, whereby officers often have to get themselves and their dogs up and down the outside of buildings, or even boats, using abseiling skills. The dogs are trained to cope with being tied to their handlers, via a harness, in order to achieve this kind of operation.

Labradors, alongside Spaniels, are trained to find specific scents. These include drugs, both hidden and being carried on a person in public; cash (banknotes); explosives; firearms; human remains and blood. Explosives search dogs work exclusively in bomb detection. All dogs can be called to operate calmly and happily in crime scenes, buildings, open spaces, vehicles, vessels, aircraft and transport infrastructure centres such as stations and bus terminals, and often accompany officers who are executing search warrants.

The police dog team of Sergeant Martin Proctor and his handsome black Labrador Dylan was awarded the Queen's Gallantry Medal in 1988 for exemplary bravery following an incident on the London Underground. In the summer of 2014, Sergeant Proctor retired after 36 years as a police dog handler, and Dylan, after eight years of sniffing duties, also bowed out for some well-earned rest and playtime. Part of their annual beat had always been ensuring the grounds of the All England Lawn Tennis Club were safe during Wimbledon fortnight. Working in the England Garden Party atmosphere for two weeks each year was such a contrast to normal explosive detection work that Sergeant Proctor deliberately chose to retire after the Championships. For a self-respecting retriever, Wimbledon is absolute heaven, with its secret cache of lost balls and rabbit-shaped furry camera microphones. 'He's extremely playful. That's what makes him such a strong dog. It's all fun to him,' said Sergeant Proctor. 'There's a giant tennis ball under a glass floor panel in the museum and let's just say he gets VERY interested in trying to get at that! We both love it.' Fellow behind-the-scenes staff at the tournament responded in kind: Dylan was one very popular dog. His last day on the beat saw him more fêted than your average champion. As he carried out his final search of the grounds ahead of the day's play, Dylan was mobbed with presents, photo requests and affectionate pats. Camera crews ran backwards to catch him in his handsome

Day-Glo harness and he duly lay down, rolled over and offered his tummy for a tickle.

'I couldn't ask for a nicer dog. Each police dog is independently licensed and I was told he wouldn't make it when he was young, but I've had dogs since 1988 and he's the best I've ever owned,' said Sergeant Proctor. 'We took a shine to each other straightaway. He's got a lovely temperament, but when he works, he clicks on and just searches. He's the ultimate pro. We're a team and we're going to miss all this.'

Police dogs work under several occupational hazards. First, they are the 'shield' for their handler, being at the epicentre of an explosion should they detect and set off a bomb, or on the frontline of gangsters involved in illegal goods trafficking. Second, if they become renowned for their success in thwarting criminals, such as drug smugglers, they themselves become 'Wanted' by the bad guys and have a price slapped on their head. For example, in an article in the *Telegraph* in 2013, Boss, a Labrador who helps lead police to stashes of drugs within the vast slum cities or favelas in Brazil, was named as the most wanted sniffer dog in Brazil. A powerful drug kingpin was said to have issued a 'death order' against the eager young Labrador, who had led police officers to a haul of more than 1.5 tonnes of drugs within twelve months. In October 2012, Boss was assigned nine protection officers after the police intercepted a message on the radio from a gang leader in the Manguinhos favela with an order to 'target Brownie' – a reference to Boss. Nine months later, in July 2013, he was still at work, uncovering 6,919 packets of cocaine worth more than £300,000 during an operation in the Favela do Rola on the west side of Rio. He also sniffed out 236 packets of cannabis, 14 blocks of cannabis and a stash of automatic weapons.

The scenario is not exclusive to Brazil, though. In Colombia, police guards were monitoring food for Agata, a champion drug-truffler, for poison. In 2007, a report in the *New Straits Times* in Malaysia told of death threats issued against sniffer dogs Lucky and Flo, whose personal expertise lay in detecting pirate CDs and DVDs.

If you've travelled around the United States by Amtrak train, the chances are you've seen a K-9 at work. Strategically deployed at stations throughout the system and involved in up to 1,000 train trips a month, the Amtrak Police Department K-9 teams provide a psychological and physical deterrent to potential threats from explosives. Up to 50 bomb detection teams – which translates into one handler and his Labrador per team – play a proactive role in the prevention of terrorism. At least a dozen of the teams are certified 'vapour-wake' dogs, which are trained to detect the smell of a suicide bomber, i.e. to determine the smell of explosives left in the wake of a person as they pass by. As Captain Deborah Myers of the unit says, 'The dogs are very dependable. They're more dependable than any piece of equipment . . . I have a dog there, it's a safe area.'

For explosives detection, the dogs begin training from 13 weeks of age, and it includes a year-long stint in prison. During an 11-week training programme at either the Auburn University Canine Detection Training Centre in Alabama or the Transportation Security Administration facility at Lackland Air Force Base, in Texas, the dogs have a lot of fun playing hide and seek with their favourite toys and tennis balls – exercises which are canny sessions in teaching odour recognition. During that time, they are partnered with a handler. The dog is the nose; the handler is the eyes and brain, taught to recognise changes in their dog's behaviour as a response to 'alerting' on a potential threat. This could be a tail signal, a head held high or 'acting stealthy', like they're sneaking up on some prey.

There has to be a lot of trust between dog and handler. Those that don't excel over 11 weeks of training don't make the cut. A lot of factors make a good explosives detection dog, says John Pearce from the Canine Detection Research Institute: 'a lot of play, a lot of desire and motivation to hunt. It's like a big game of hide and seek, looking for their toy or their tennis ball.'

All this is a far cry from my own dogs. To all intents and purposes, despite being a crossbreed, Maggi looks exactly like a Labrador. The only characteristic that gives away her mixed genes is her ears. She has the unmistakable 'r'-shaped ears of a Collie; she also has the sheepdog head tilt. At first glance most people assume she is a pure-bred Labrador, but get to know her and you recognise the obsessive compulsive attributes of the Collie.

Maggi has the most incredible coat of any dog I know. A rich brown that borders on red during the winter and bleaches to strawberry blonde in the summer. Where Inca's life was largely dominated by her love of food, Maggi is obsessed with tennis balls. I don't mean in an occasional play kind of way, but an OCD crazy kind of love. She could chase a ball all day and stare at one for even longer. I often used to wonder if she had merely confused it for a sheep. A friend of Marina's once bought her a tub of 200 multi-coloured tennis balls, after which our house resembled one of those children's ball parks.

Wherever Maggi went, there was sure to be a tennis ball.

Apart from my parents' dog, Maggi was the only other dog that Inca ever really liked. Inca never really liked other dogs; I could probably say that Inca disliked most other dogs – she was more into people. I'm not sure if it was because she was bullied by the Collies on the island, or because she wasn't properly socialised, but Inca just really wasn't into other dogs. She would crouch down, holding her head close to the ground in a form of submission while baring her teeth in a snarl. She would usually give the other dog a couple of seconds to read her behaviour before letting rip with her snapping jaws.

At first it was quite funny. It seemed such unlikely Labrador behaviour, particularly from a female, but her aggression towards other dogs became more and more pronounced. She seemed to focus all her doggy angst, rage and hatred towards particular breeds. At the top of her death list were, somewhat unexpectedly, Boxers.

Personally, I've always liked Boxers, but Inca HATED them. If she spotted one, and she could identify one from several hundred metres, she would chase it down and attack it, or try to, until one of her seizures felled her to the ground. Poor Inca.

Maggi took all of this in her stride. Maggi wasn't really into other dogs either. If she could choose anything as a best friend it would be a tennis ball. Though loyal and kind, Maggi isn't really into people either. Maybe it is the Collie in her, but she rarely tolerates more than a fleeting stroke on her head. She certainly never likes a cuddle.

Maggi and Inca had a strange dynamic of affable acceptance. Although I like to think they were inseparable, I'm not sure either of them was really that concerned when they were separated. We would sometimes divide them between my parents and Marina's parents to share the burden.

Children was as much of a shock for Inca and Maggi as it was for us. Ludo was our first born. He arrived on 9 December and he turned our world upside down, for the better of course, but it meant we were pretty dizzy for a while.

Both Marina and I had read plenty of books on the effect children can have on family pets, particularly if they are used to being fussed over. Maggi and Inca had had several years of playing the role of our surrogate children and now they were about to be usurped by a screaming child. I prepared myself for jealousy and angst, but the dogs took Ludo's arrival in their stride. In fact, Ludo's arrival had an unexpected effect on her.

The only time I saw anything verging on jealousy from either of the dogs was the first day we took Ludo to the park. He was barely a week old and we bundled him into his pram and took him to Hyde Park. The dogs sniffed around his pram in curiosity; neither of them could really understand what this screaming, pooing little thing was. Eventually Inca stood in front of the pram and began to scrape mud and leaves into the air, and straight into the pram. This was no accident. I had never seen her do it before and it was so well directed that I'm sure it was a sign of her frustration.

Yet Inca loved both of our children, Ludo and Iona, and having them around seemed to spur her ailing body on. Ludo would squeal with delight whenever he saw her, placing his face close to hers and staring into her eyes. Nothing gave me greater pleasure than seeing the children and the dogs together.

Having children gave me the final insight into the Labrador as a family pet. Some would argue that this is their greatest role. Think of a family pet and, more often than not, you'll imagine a Labrador.

The Labrador has all of the perfect traits. It is true there are many breeds well suited to children, but the Labrador has the added bonus of being both tolerant and wanting to please. It is this double whammy that makes them a trustworthy choice.

Of course, no one can ever trust any animal 100 per cent, but I'd argue that when it comes to trust and Labradors, that percentage is in the high 90s.

Inca would sit there as the children squeezed and poked her. To be honest, I think she enjoyed the physical contact. I have a wonderful photograph of Ludo sitting on her back while Inca lies care-free on the lawn.

I suppose we need to ask ourselves what we want from a family pet. I'd argue you need calmness, happiness, a willingness to please, a team player, tolerance and, above all, loyalty. A family dog is a projection of your core values. For me, a family dog says I am not the most important person or thing in this family. It is about shared responsibility.

In many ways Inca became a third pair of eyes on the children. I'm not sure she would have done anything if something serious ever actually happened, but I found her a reassuring presence. Maggi tolerated the children, but she was never that into them. I imagine that might be the Collie blood in her. Given half a chance, she would happily round them up, but from the beginning we'd notice Maggi slinking off upstairs whenever the children were about.

Inca, on the other hand, gained a spring in her step – though I still suspect it had something to do with the shower of food that descended from the children's highchairs.

Inca didn't just gain two children when Ludo and Iona came along – she also gained a couple of kilos.

CHAPTER ELEVEN

LABS OF WAR

When I was a boy I remember reading the stories about the 'dogs of war'; these were the tales of the maverick mercenaries who acted as guns for hire, working in war zones from West Africa to Central America.

As a boy, the 'dogs of war' were the real-life heroes of Boys' Own adventures. It never occurred to me to question why they were called dogs let alone challenge the morals of their escapades.

'Cry "Havoc!", and let slip the dogs of war' comes from Shakespeare's *Julius Caesar* (Act 3, Scene 1, line 273, to be precise). It was uttered by Mark Antony shortly after the assassination of Caesar. There is an ongoing debate about whether the Bard's use of the phrase 'dogs of war' was a metaphor for soldiers rather than four-legged warriors straining at the leash to snatch at the spoils of battle, but scholars agree that there is precedent for the literal translation, and dogs have been used in warfare since ancient times.

So where do Labradors come into this?

As early as 4000 BC, the Egyptians prized dogs for their role as sentries, hunting companions and guard dogs – and as snarling offensive weapons to let loose on their enemies. The ancient Egyptian word for dog was *iwiw*, which is an onomatopoeic reference to its bark. Hyper-alert and vigilant, the dog was well suited to act as a mobile alarm system, boosted by its acute sense of hearing and smell.

If you think about it, it's a great bit of kit. There are numerous depictions in paintings and murals of ancient Egyptian breeds that resemble modern Salukis, Greyhounds and Mastiffs. Preserved remains of leather collars and carved *stelae* stones reveal the names given to these dogs: Brave One, Reliable and Good Herdsman – the names give a tiny insight into the dogs' reliability and fortitude. Whatever warlike purpose dogs have served – from sentry duty through to sophisticated detection – they have a long history of being employed in some, often noble, capacity.

In *The Odyssey*, Homer's dogs appear as hunters capable of squaring up to savage animals like lions and bears. They are depicted as guards for public buildings and for valuable herds of sheep. Canine fighting skills encouraged the resourceful Greeks, Babylonians and Assyrians to dress their dogs in armour, complete with spikes, to ensure the dogs could participate in hand-to-hand, or paw-to-paw, combat. That was, of course, before the invention of gunpowder.

As the nature of warfare evolved, so did the role dogs that could play. In the eighteenth and nineteenth centuries, Native Americans used dogs as sentries and pack animals to carry their belongings. In the Russo-Japanese War of 1904 to 1905, the Russian Army trained ambulance dogs. In the Spanish-Moroccan War of 1919 to 1926, dogs were schooled to run along the front lines to draw enemy fire and give away the enemy's gun positions. The potential of a dog's trainability seemed limitless.

Faithful, loyal and agile, the dog seemed a natural choice.

The role of ambulance dog showed how man and canine can work well together even in high-stress jobs. Often the dogs would be used to search for wounded personnel under the cover of night, within a marked territory on the battlefield – injured soldiers often hide themselves from further danger, making themselves invisible to both friend and foe.

A dog's acute sense of hearing enables them to detect the sound of a wounded man's breath or groans even when they are inaudible to the human ear; their super-sensitive nose can ferret out the scent of a man lying in a concealed place, perhaps unconscious. The ambulance dog works in several ways; the dog can be trained to return to his handler and lead him to the wounded man, he can be taught to bark to communicate his location, or to work on a long lead to lead a human medic to the right spot. We've all seen images of Red Cross dogs proudly wearing saddles with pockets to store bandages, first-aid dressings and very often a flask of stimulant (or brandy). In the early twentieth century English ambulance dogs wore a light saddle marked with the Geneva Cross with a loud bell hanging from a leather collar. The Russians equipped their ambulance dogs with small lanterns as well as bells. There are many depictions of Labradors working as ambulance dogs, too.

It is strange but true that the qualities that make a good

soldier are as readily found in a dog (of particular breeds) as in a human. Candidates preparing for interviews for roles in the military services are advised to stress personality traits such as courage, dependability in the line of duty, enthusiasm, decisiveness, unselfishness, integrity, loyalty, a good spirit and a willingness to follow orders and strategies. Many a breed of dog boasts that package of qualities. In 1808, Lord Byron wrote in an epitaph for his beloved Newfoundland dog, Boatswain,

> *In life the firmest friend,*
> *The first to welcome, foremost to defend,*
> *Whose honest heart is still his master's own*
> *Who labours, fights, lives, breathes for him alone.*

Lord Byron was summing up what we dog owners have always known, but his observations also confirm why dogs working in war zones have become canine war heroes themselves.

Many a poet and statesman has been moved to pay tribute to the dog as ultimate wingman, a living creature you want next to you in the trenches or the foxhole. Most famously, Napoleon recalled this cameo scene in his memoirs: 'I walked over the battlefield and among the slain, a poodle killed bestowing a last lick upon his dead friend's face. Never had anything on any battlefield caused me a like emotion.'

In the theatre of war, soldiers say a dog is much more than a best friend; the dog is both an extension of yourself and your guardian angel. So when does the Labrador Retriever fit into the war dog tradition? As the breed was only officially recognised with Kennel Club status in 1903, it is to the Great War and twentieth-century wars that the Labrador's qualities first came to notice. The very same traits that attracted the Newfoundland cod fisherman and later the British aristocracy would lead the Labrador firmly into the fold of battle.

Field-Marshal Haig acknowledged the essential role of dogs in the British Army in his final despatch from the First World War. The introduction of trained dogs to the war effort was solely due to one Lieutenant Colonel Edwin Hauteville Richardson, who fervently believed in the vital role that a well-trained dog could play in combat alongside troops in the trenches. Were it not for him, dogs may never have been used by the British Army.

Edwin Richardson's story is pretty moving. The youngest son of a farmer, he grew up an animal lover. At school, he learnt about dogs being trained on the continent for military purposes and decided to find out more. He studied canine history and the use of dogs in warfare by the ancient Greeks and by the French during Napoleon's era, and later went to Sandhurst military academy. On passing out, he and his wife bought farm-land on the east coast of Scotland and began to experiment with training dogs for military purposes. He had been inspired after observing a curious incident in 1895 when, shooting on a friend's moor in Scotland, he noticed a German man buying a sheepdog from a shepherd. It transpired the man had been sent by the German government to buy a large number of Collies for the German Army, because they were so useful in searching and returning to a given spot. From 1900 onwards, Richardson began training dogs as 'ambulance dogs' with the help of officers at nearby army camps. He travelled to Russia and Germany to pick up tips on how dogs were used by police and army forces on the continent. His dogs – initially mostly Airedale Terriers – proved useful comrades in these experimental scenarios, by day and by night, prompting officers to request an official recognition of war dogs. Several attempts were made to persuade the Army of the potential usefulness of dogs in protecting ammunition dumps and factories against enemy saboteurs, but Richardson and his supporters made no headway in getting a commission. However, in the early years of the Great War, and with no official military dogs attached to the British Army, the War Office suddenly contacted Richardson to request that he form an official training school for war dogs.

In 1916, in response to a request from the Royal Artillery, Colonel Richardson began to train dogs as messengers. He trained two dogs, Wolf and Prince, and sent them to the front line. The dogs' ability to take vital messages about reinforcements, artillery and positioning during heavy bombardments was perfect. The idea was for a soldier to attach a message to the dog's collar, send the dog 'over the top' of the trench, and expect the dog to convey the message a few kilometres away within minutes. It worked.

I used to do the same with Inca. Marina and I used to spend holidays and long weekends in an idyllic little cottage high on the cliffs overlooking Putsborough Sands on the North Devon coast. I used to use it as a writer's den. I would sit at the window overlooking the ocean and Lundy Island beyond while Marina would lie on the beach below and read.

We used the dogs to send messages between one another. I

would place a note in a plastic bag tied to their collars and send them down the steep cliff. It worked a treat. The dogs became so good at it that I ended up sending ice cream down to her, or at least I did it once . . . until Inca worked out how to get the ice cream out of the bag and into her mouth. Like I say, Labradors love food.

Fortunately for the army, their dogs were used to transport messages rather than food.

A source material on these highly trained messenger dogs, which is in the archive at the University of Edinburgh, reads: 'One of their first tasks was to carry a message four miles to brigade headquarters from the front line through a smoke barrage, a task completed within an hour. It soon became clear that dogs were faster, steadier, more nimble across shell holes and muddy terrain, and more difficult to spot than human messengers. The two dogs were trailblazers. With Wolf and Prince having proved the usefulness of dogs at the front, demand for more messenger dogs grew and Lt-Col Richardson was asked by the War Office to establish his British War Dog School in 1917.'

Individual officers began to request dogs for sentry and patrol duties, as well as in messenger roles. The Richardsons sold up and moved to Shoeburyness, in Essex, where the Colonel established the first training centre for British military working dogs.

Richardson trained hundreds of dogs, mostly gathered from rescue centres. Not all dogs made the grade, though; some were too flaky to adopt a disciplined, task-specific mindset. Just like the soldiers, the army required focused, dedicated candidates. Each dog underwent intensive training for weeks to 'go over the top', cross tricky terrain, swim canals and leap over barbed wire entanglements, all the while ignoring the whistling bullets and explosions around them. Demand grew. All over Britain, police were instructed to send strays of any breed to the school. The War Office even appealed to the public to donate their own pets.

Now I am a patriotic soul. I have even spent a small amount of time in the military myself, as an officer cadet in the University Royal Naval Unit, but there is no way I would ever donate my dog to the war effort, however dire the situation. Some of the letters accompanying the donated family pets are heartbreaking. One lady wrote: 'I have given my husband and my sons, and now that he too is required, I give my dog.'

Can you imagine this kind of selflessness today?

Richardson's training regime at the British War Dog School encouraged kindness, gentleness and reward. It also acclimatised the dogs to loud battlefront conditions by feeding them amid similar noise, working them through mock trenches and encouraging them to run towards the crackle of rifle fire. It was also designed to build up the bond between dog and handler.

The nature of warfare was quick to change, and soon war became a far dirtier proposition.

'Keeper Davis talked of his dogs, Joe and Lizzard, who could cover three miles at night in twenty minutes, and they are just the same on any front that we go to.' Keeper Brooks, reporting on one of his dogs, Tom, spoke of how the dog was gassed and hit by shrapnel but was quite well again after a fortnight's rest. Keeper Swankie's dog, Ginger, suffered from shell shock but eventually recovered and was back on duty, and 'able to cover a mile in just three and a half minutes.'

By the end of the First World War more than 20,000 dogs had served on the front line, 7,000 of which had been family pets before war had broken out.

Lt Col Richardson is quoted: 'The trained dog considers himself highly honoured by his position as a servant of His Majesty, and renders no reluctant service. From my observation along this line I have, in fact, come to the conclusion that a dog trained to some definite work is happier than the average loafing dog, no matter how kindly the latter may be treated. I certainly found it to be the case with the army dogs.'

Although many owners of family pets may find this hard to read, these observations do in fact concur with those of many animal behaviourists, who conclude that a busy dog is a happy dog.

During the same period, Red Cross institutions in many countries employed Mercy Dogs to identify and comfort the wounded men on the front lines, but it is Richardson's Tactical Dog programme that formed the lasting legacy. Dogs used in war are now officially titled Military Working Dogs (MWDs) in the United Kingdom. The Defence Animal Centre in Melton Mowbray, Leicestershire, which opened in 1946, is home to the Joint Service Dog School which trains approximately 300 dogs a year and offers 22 handler courses, ranging from explosive detection to search and protection. It offers the most sophisticated dog training in the world. The high demand for these dogs prompted the army to consolidate five MWD squadrons into the first Military Working Dog regiment in March 2010. The regiment has nearly 300 soldiers and 200 dogs, supporting world-wide operations.

Richardson's book, *British War Dogs*, was used as a training manual by the United States' Quartermaster Corps in 1942, when it started its first official K-9 Army. Today, the American services have 2,800 working dogs, divided into four categories – including one category of specialised search dogs (SSDs) starring our friend, the Labrador Retriever. The Lab has proven invaluable in locating improvised explosive devices, the number-one killer of coalition forces in Iraq and Afghanistan.

What makes a Labrador suited to work in a warzone? In a world of technologically sophisticated weapons detection systems, the Lab's best assets are its nose and ears. They reign supreme on the ground. An average dog smells 50 to 100 times more sensitively than an average person and they remember smells better than things they have seen.

I have seen this first hand on the course of hundreds, if not thousands, of dog walks over the years – the daily sniffathon, as I call it. Can you imagine if humans greeted one another by sniffing one another's bottoms?

The physiological reason for this is that dogs' olfactory centres consist of approximately two billion olfactory receptors compared to 40 million in humans. Labradors are particularly brilliant at tracking ground scent (as opposed to airborne), thanks to an extraordinary ability to distinguish one individual scent and follow it despite thousands of competing smells.

As far as the ears go, dogs have a broad hearing spectrum which allows them to hear frequencies as high as 35,000 cycles per second (Hz) compared to humans' upper limit of 20,000 Hz. Their ability to hear high-pitched sounds means, they are able to detect incoming shells before a soldier can. They can close their inner ear to filter out background noise and focus on a task at hand. Erect ears are better than floppy or fold-over ears, which is why German Shepherds are particularly good for scout work rather than sniffer duties.

In general terms, dogs are near-sighted, but their sense of smell and hearing compensate during bright daylight hours. It is a fact that dogs don't see as well as humans during the day, but from dusk through the night to dawn they have superior vision because in the retina of their eyes there are more rods (responsible for light sensibility) than cones (responsible for colour), which respond better to dim light.

Temperament, as well as physiology, influences whether a dog makes a good war worker, and this factor became more important as gradually the employment of dogs became increasingly specialised. During World War Two, Doberman Pinschers were initially the preferred dog for the Marines. When the military changed tack and began preparing dogs more as scout dogs than sentry and messenger dogs, they had to look beyond Dobermans, who were excellent sentries but were too excitable and skittish on the battlefield. Bloodhounds have excellent scenting ability but they are too noisy to be used as tracker dogs. So German Shepherds, with their famously stable temperament, emerged as first-choice combat dog. By the Vietnam War, Labrador Retrievers were the number-one choice as trackers because they could be trained to be quiet. A dog's ability to withstand climatic extremes also has to be taken into consideration. In Vietnam, the dog handlers were warned to expect losses due to heatstroke.

Today dogs are celebrated as war heroes. The Animals in War

Memorial at Brook Gate, Park Lane, in London, is a powerful monument to all the animals that served, suffered and died alongside the British, Commonwealth and Allied forces in the wars and conflicts of the twentieth century. The monument comprises two different levels separated by a dominating wall. On the lower level, two laden mules struggle on towards a flight of steps that leads through the wall that symbolises the war experience. On the other side, a bronze horse and dog stand facing into the gardens, bearing witness to the loss of their comrades and symbolising hope for the future.

There would be no accolade for these dogs of war were it not for the steadfast companionship they enjoy with their handlers who have proudly told of their exploits down through generations. And so it is that in war there are countless heart-warming stories of dogs' loyalty, devotion, bravery and courage as their role evolved. Among these, it is fascinating to look at where and how the Labrador features throughout twentieth- and twenty-first-century warfare.

The Labrador is first notable as a mascot dog. There is a wonderful photograph of the then Wing Commander Johnnie Johnson (he later became Air Vice Marshal CB, CBE, DSO & Two Bars, DFC & Bar) standing in front of the propeller of his Spitfire, cigarette between his lips, greeting his beloved black Labrador, Sally, the squadron mascot. Johnson was one of the most celebrated RAF flying aces of the Second World War. He flew alongside Sir Douglas Bader and, with a tally of 34 victories over Messerschmitt Bf 109s and 20 Focke-Wulf Fw 190s, emerged as the highest-scoring Western Allied fighter ace against the German Luftwaffe.

Clearly, a black Labrador was the fashionable squadron accessory. The iconic example of this is the Dambuster dog, a male
black Labrador Retriever belonging to the legendary Wing
Commander Guy Gibson, whose presence is still felt today at
RAF Scampton, Lincolnshire, where he is buried.

Guy Gibson was the first Commanding Officer of the Royal
Air Force's 617 Squadron who led the 1943 Dam Busters raid
– immortalised in the film starring Michael Redgrave and
Richard Todd – which resulted in the destruction of two large
dams in the Ruhr area. He was awarded the Victoria Cross,
but lost his life later in the war at the age of 24, having under-
taken more than 170 operations. In a biography of his life,
Dambuster: a Life of Guy Gibson VC, Susan Ottaway describes
the memorable role of Gibson's black Labrador called Nigger.
(The name was commonly given to dogs before it became
taboo in the late twentieth century. To avoid offence, I shall
refer to Gibson's beloved dog as N.) In 1941, Guy and his wife
Eve acquired a puppy who was 'full of character'. N went
everywhere with Guy, having beers bought for him in the
officers' mess (no one's drink was safe with N around), and
even accompanying his master into the cockpit on flights. N
would curl up on the floor and sleep, quite unconcerned about
the chugging noise and action that surrounded him. Life as a
commander of 106 and later 617 Squadron was stressful and
lonely. Gibson was the boss; he couldn't spend the evenings
with the other lads, and while living away from Eve during
the war years, he came to rely on N for companionship. They
would go for long walks in the grounds of a nearby country
estate and sometimes go out on a boat together on the estate

lake. They would attend social occasions together, as commander
and squadron mascot. N became quite a hardened drinker. He
was adored by the rest of the squadron and even wore on his
collar an Iron Cross that had been crafted for him. Man and
dog were devoted to each other.

During preparations for the 'bouncing bomb' Dambuster
raid, which took place on the night of 16–17 May 1943, it was
decided Guy would coordinate the operation by radio. He
would use certain code words to simplify the procedure. Words
such as 'Dinghy' and 'Nigger' would signify that the targets
had been destroyed. 'Nigger' (Morse code: -. .. --. --. . .-.) was
the code word Gibson would use to confirm the breach of the
Möhne Dam. As Susan Ottaway relates, 'It was, perhaps, a
horrible irony that the word 'Nigger' should have been chosen
to mean the destruction of a target, for, on the night of 15
May, as Guy was writing out his operation orders, his beloved
dog, N, was killed by a car outside the main gates at Scampton.
Group Captain Whitworth brought Guy the awful news and
told him that N's body had been taken to the guard room. It
is not hard to imagine how Guy must have felt at that moment.
N had been his faithful companion since he first came to live
with him as a puppy down in Kent. They had shared so much
and, when times were hard for Guy, N had always been there
with a friendly greeting for his master. The dog's death was a
devastating blow for Guy, and, coming as it did, the day before
the most important mission he had ever flown, was a disaster.
Guy was, however, a true professional in his work and was
determined not to let this personal tragedy affect the raid. His
time for grieving would have to wait until the raid had been

satisfactorily carried out. Knowing that some of the crews might regard N's death as a bad omen, Guy asked that they should not be told until after their return.

The next morning Guy discreetly arranged the burial of his dog. He did not want to do it himself but asked that it be carried out at midnight that night, the precise time he was due to be over the target. Ottaway reports that he spoke to a Flight Sergeant in the station workshop and asked him to build a coffin for N, but the man refused to do that for a dog and a row ensued, with Guy losing his temper. The burial was carried out by Flight Sergeant Powell, 617's disciplinary NCO, to the letter of Gibson's instructions, and at midnight his little four-legged friend was laid to rest. Marked much later by a proper stone, the carefully tended little grave remains to this day on the grass outside the original 617 Squadron offices at RAF Scampton. As history relates, the mission was successful but the squadron suffered loss of crew. On 18 May the men of 617 Squadron were given special leave but Gibson stayed in his office, which overlooked N's freshly dug grave, and, full of emotion himself, wrote letters to the families of those who had not returned.

The Labrador picked to play the part of N in the 1954 film *The Dam Busters* was an army dog, trained in mine detection. He had never been involved in film work before but was hailed a natural actor in the role, obediently following the director's instruction. However, in one scene, he had to trot past the place where the real N was buried. He dug in his heels and could not be persuaded to go near the grave. He couldn't even be dragged past it. Since his death in 1943 there have been many sightings of the ghost of N, so could the actor dog detect something? In

November 2011, it was reported that paranormal investigators, given special permission to stake out the RAF base which is now home to the Red Arrows, claimed that the spectre of the dog's spirit tried to communicate to them as they have picked up activity on their electronic detection equipment. And so the legend lives on . . .

The Red Arrows' first mascot was also a Labrador – a golden-coated dog called Dusty. He belonged to Squadron Leader Henry Prince, an aerobatic display pilot who flew at Red 7 in the original line-up in 1965. Dusty was often observed at his master's feet during briefings and occasionally ventured into the cockpit. He was photographed wearing flying helmet and goggles with his paws over the side of the Folland Gnat jet trainer. Sadly, like N, Dusty met a tragic end on the eve of a milestone event in his master's life. He died on the day before the Red Arrows' first ever display in May 1965, hit by the propeller of an aircraft as he followed at the heels of an airman who had rushed out to speak to the Chief Flying Instructor. Dusty was buried at RAF Fairford in a small grave on the north side of the airfield, marked by a gravestone and a white picket fence. On 24 June 2014, a group of children from Kempsford Primary School, whose parents are all serving members of the RAF, cleaned up Dusty's resting place as part of the celebrations to mark the 50th display season of the Red Arrows.

Labradors came into their own as serving war dogs towards the end of World War Two leading into the Vietnam War, which waged from 1955 to the fall of Saigon in 1975.

The British government rejected US requests to send troops to Vietnam, but even so there was significant indirect practical support from Britain, much of which went under the radar. The contribution that involved Labradors was in offering the US Special Forces training in jungle warfare using tracker dogs. During World War Two, Britain had initiated successful 'recce' patrols as a tactic for finding pockets of Japanese soldiers hidden on the Pacific Islands. They trained their tracker dogs at the Jungle Warfare School in Malaysia. In 1966 – eleven years into the Vietnam War – Britain allowed the United States to begin training 14 tracker teams there as well. Thirty dogs supplied by the British made up these first 14 teams. The 63rd Infantry Platoon Combat Tracker team, for example, received Bruce, Lucky and Sambo – valued comrades who lived in well-constructed kennels with concrete runs, wash points, drainage, chain-wire enclosures and secure covered accommodation. The dogs were well looked after. During World War Two, US soldiers had elevated the status of dogs, listing their canine comrades as wounded or killed in the compilation of casualties with accompanying remarks stressing their courage or devotion. This practice was forbidden by army regulations, but the bold defiance demonstrates the immediate respect held by the men responsible for handling the dogs. They agreed that a dog's action was often the difference between life and death for a platoon.

A distinguishing feature of Vietcong strategy was to ambush and then disappear quickly into the night. The US and Army of the Republic of Viet Nam (ARVN) soldiers needed a means of tracking the Vietcong back to their enclave where the larger force could be eliminated. The purpose of the tracker team is to find retreating or evading enemy troops, but not to engage with them. 'Locate and wait' was the name of the game. Black or yellow Labrador Retrievers were preferred because of their super-sensitive noses and their strong ability to scent on the ground. A tracker dog is trained specifically to follow only one scent, which it learns by sniffing a footprint or blood spot, giving the dog a unique signature smell to follow. Ideally they would be deployed within a three-hour window of known enemy presence, but in certain conditions a scent trail could be followed up to 24 hours later. The tracker dogs were able to detect enemy soldiers with ease because the Asian diet was based on rice while the American diet was based on wheat. The resulting body odours are quite different to the dog's keen nose. Tracker dogs are not taught to attack or to alert to booby traps or tripwires, though many did through natural instinct.

Private Peter Haran of the Royal Australian Infantry wrote a memoir about his time as a War Dog Operative in South Vietnam teamed with his Labrador Kelpie cross, Caesar. Life in the J – as the Aussies referred to the jungle – was stressful, and in *Trackers* Haran brings it to life complete with Aussie slang and gallows humour. A tracker team of dog and handler had to be on standby for rapid deployment. Haran's description of a memorable sortie is pretty vivid:

> *A dog team was called for. It was my turn, so I grabbed my combat gear, collected Caesar and went to the 2 RAR helicopter landing pad – codenamed 'Eagle Farm'. There were three of us. My cover man, a machine gunner, myself and of course, Caesar. We boarded a Huey (UH-1 Iroquois helicopter), took off, and within ten minutes we arrived at the D Coy position. We quickly deplaned and were taken to the*

contact site. There was a great deal of blood scattered on the sandy ground as well as streaked along some bushes. My cover man said 'I'm ready when you are'. The Pl Commander (who had been commanding 12 Pl for only one week) gave the order to commence the track. Caesar began his track at a fast pace and the tracking team followed at the end of his leash. 12 Pl did not patrol on the track, they were aware of the land mines and preferred to move off the sides of the track. My cover man and I had no choice but to honour where Caesar wanted to go, and he wanted to go on the track where the strongest enemy sign was. We patrolled for a couple of hundred metres, when we came upon a T junction in the track.

This was a dangerous situation and I willed Caesar to point. He did not. Instead, Caesar came straight back to me and sat on my foot. He had never done this before. We were now stopped and exposed in the middle of an open track. The next thing, there was a terrible explosion and we discovered that the Pl Commander had stepped on a mine. It exploded and blew off both his legs. An engineer splinter team arrived and began clearing the mine blast area with their counter-mine equipment. Once cleared, the casualties were treated and evacuated by DUSTOFF medical helicopter. The two sappers then went in front of Peter and continued their sweep for mines along the track which lead to the T junction. At the T junction the sappers removed a large anti-tank mine and four M16 anti-personnel 'jumping jacks'. Caesar had never received any training in mine and explosive detection, but he was suspicious of what he found at the T junction

*and for good measure, came back and sat on my foot so that
I would not continue toward the danger. Soon after, we were
all airlifted by helicopter back to our base at Nui Dat. That
was the worst day I was to experience during my tour of
duty. That day haunted me then, and continues to do so to
this day.*

At the end of his tour of duty, Haran had to hand Caesar over
to another dog handler. The farewell was heartbreaking:

*In the last day, I went up and I actually spoke to him through
the cage. I said, 'This is the way they run the war – I'm
going, you're staying. I don't want you to forget me 'cause I
won't ever forget you'. And I turned and I walked away. He
had his bowl in his mouth, expecting food – and I heard the
bowl hit the concrete. And as that happened, I felt this ton
of lead just fall straight through me from the top to the
bottom.*

Later, in 1970, Caesar was retired to the Australian Embassy in
Saigon. Haran thought he'd long said his goodbye to his faithful
dog, but on 3 October 1987, he had tucked into the beer with
some mates after the march in the Welcome Home Parade when
someone pressed something into his hand, saying 'This is for
you'. Haran took the item to a private spot and had a 'cathartic
experience'. The item was a silver identity disc engraved D6NO3
CAESAR that had hung from his collar during his lifetime. Dog
and handler were reunited.

It won't surprise you to hear that Caesar was a Labrador.

It is hard to imagine the Labrador, from its ice-wrapped origins in Newfoundland, working diligently in the steaming, triple-canopy jungle environment of Southeast Asia, but their genetic docility remained strong and they could tolerate the heat reasonably well. They would be trained for eight months, starting at the age of two, and would be expected to work in the combat zone for six years or so. The relationship between dog and handler had to be strong as the detection alerts were silent and subtle – a tail wagging, a raising of the head or twitching of an ear. The handler would be vigilant in spotting any change in behaviour that might not be recognisable to others. The Labrador's gentleness and friendliness also allowed for short transition periods between different handlers, practical in the high-stress arena of war.

In 1968, the US Army started training their own tracker dogs at Fort Gordon, Georgia. In 1968, they sent 10 tracker teams to Vietnam; in 1969, another 10, scattered throughout South Vietnam. On paper, the tracker strategy looked good, but the flaw was that the tracker teams themselves were sometimes ambushed, because dogs trained to follow a ground scent weren't trained to alert when the enemy was near. Nevertheless, the Labrador was as immersed in war experience as was its human comrades. Photographs show Labradors poised to jump from helicopters, standing guard while their handler sleeps, stalking through the jungle, sleeping with their noses on their handlers' legs, wearing an M1 combat helmet for a photograph or – sadly – resting in dog cemeteries.

When the war was over, the tracker dogs were left behind. There was no precedent for this: dogs had been demilitarised and brought home after World War Two. Like tanks and other specific items of war, the dogs were classed as 'equipment' and would be left behind. The news that most of the 4,000 dogs were to be handed over to the Army of the Republic of Viet Nam – who did not want them – prompted high emotion. The Vietnamese considered the black Labrador trackers bad luck. The dogs were large compared to their new handlers and many were scared of them. One platoon, aware that the Vietnamese had no affection for the dogs, was reported to have put their dogs down rather than leave them to an unknown fate. The prevailing belief was that the dogs became another source of 'walking protein' for the ARVN troops.

In 1970, when the American public learnt of the decision to leave the hero war dogs in Vietnam, there was outrage. Animal lovers and politicians tried to file bills in Congress, but despite the newspaper headlines the decision was not reversed. A conciliatory gesture was announced that allowed all 'healthy' dogs to return. Out of 4,000 dogs, only 120 were transported out; 500 were listed killed in action.

Thirty years later, it was President Bill Clinton – himself a Labrador owner – who signed into law HR 5314, that the Department of Defense release old and infirm war dogs to their handlers, civilian law enforcement agencies, or other responsible civilians.

The dogs of war were reunited.

CHAPTER TWELVE

THE END OF THE INCAS

I always dreaded the end. Even from the beginning, I worried about the end. I am certainly no pessimist; on the contrary, I consider myself an optimist. A fatalist. But I have experienced the pain before. You never forget losing a dog. It haunts you.

Time waits for neither man nor dog, and one of the brutal truths of the natural order is that man outlives most other species. I always knew it would happen, but nothing really prepared me for the sudden shock.

I was on the Isle of Wight on a family holiday with our dogs, Inca and Maggi. Inca's deterioration had been rapid. At 12, she had lost full control of her back legs and even walking had become difficult. She would often collapse while eating or, worse, while relieving herself; frequently I found myself holding her while she did her business. I had to carry her in and out of the car, and soon she couldn't even get up from her bed.

To make the decision to let my best friend go was one of the hardest decisions I have ever had to make. 'Are you prolonging her life for you or for Inca?' asked my dad. It was a question he has posed countless times over the years in his capacity as a vet.

Suddenly I was not just his son but a client with his beloved dog. Dad never made the decision for me; he wanted me to decide when the time was right.

'You'll know,' he had once told me.

I was about 8 when I first experienced the pain of losing a dog: Honey, a beautiful Golden Retriever. She had belonged to my mother, Julia Foster, then a famous actress. It was the perfect love story; my mother took her beloved dog to the vet, where she met a swarthy vet who would soon become her husband and, more importantly, my father.

You see, my father is key to this whole story. The canine blood that flows through my body was inherited from him. If the Fogle family had a crest it would most certainly be of dogs. They are to our family what chocolate is to the Cadburys. Breed is irrelevant. Dogs are in the Fogle DNA. Nature AND nurture.

Honey was the first dog I knew and the first dog I lost. I can remember snapshots. I can remember her becoming old, lying in her rectangular wicker basket that sat beneath the window of my parents' bedroom. I can remember the lumps on her belly. I recall coming home from school and my parents leading me into their room. I remember lying on her lifeless body, already stiff. I sobbed. I think it was the first time I ever sobbed like that. Uncontrollable emotion that I didn't really understand. She was gone but death was still abstract. She had gone, but where to?

I remember Dad carrying her lifeless body down the stairs and it was the last time I ever saw that red-blonde coat of hers. We weren't sure where to bury her. We didn't have a garden in our London house so some friends volunteered to let us bury her in their garden in Sussex. She's still there, of course, beneath an apple tree.

Bereavement for a pet is a strange thing. I was overwhelmed with a feeling of betrayal; I had cared for and protected this dog, who in turn had showered me with loyalty and love: the unspoken bond of trust between man (and woman) and dog.

The week following her death was awful. I was a wreck. I suffered panic attacks. I couldn't stop crying. It was like losing a limb. My shadow had gone. It was like a small flame had been extinguished within. There was a yawning gap in my life.

Time is a great healer. You never forget, but the ache begins to wane.

Then there was my beloved Liberty, also a Golden Retriever. She died while I was away doing a ski season in France. And Lexington, she died while I was marooned on the island of Taransay. My mother sent me a letter to tell me the sad news. On the envelope she had written very clearly, 'OPEN IN PRIVATE'. I of course ignored her advice and opened it on camera. I promptly burst into tears. Each of those losses had been preceded by an extraordinary life. Each of those dogs had their own unique impact on me, but Inca was the most powerful. Perhaps it was because of the intensity of our relationship. Maybe it was because she was MY first dog, as opposed to our family's.

Inca was cremated. For a long time her ashes remained in a little urn at my parents' house. I couldn't bring myself to scatter them. I had always been certain that her ashes belonged on Taransay. It was her island; it was where she was at both her healthiest and happiest.

But a lot had happened in the 10 years since we had been marooned together. The island had changed hands and Inca had become a London dog. The park was more familiar to her than the wild machair of the Western Isles. So there was really only one place that she belonged: Hyde Park, where she had so many walks and where she had helped me find the love of my life.

I bought a small beech tree sapling. It is hidden in a corner of the park, close to where Marina and I had first seen one another. A tree seemed so symbolic. I could think of Inca each time I saw it.

A year after Inca had died, my parents, my sister, Marina and Ludo all walked through the park accompanied by more than a dozen dogs, including Inca's daughter, Lola, and all of her canine friends. I carried her ashes in a little bag while my mother had packed a hamper full of champagne and Bonios. We gathered around the little tree, Inca's tree, and I took her old dog tag from my pocket. I placed it low on the tree and, using a little wire, attached it to the base of the trunk. I then scattered her ashes. I placed a hanging Bonio in the tree in homage to that insatiable appetite and we raised our champagne glasses to Inca.

It was sad, but it was also uplifting. I have a photograph – perhaps one of my most precious photographs – of a lush green meadow; trees are in full leaf; it looks rich and luxurious. It is of me, Ludo and all the dogs gathered around the little tree.

It was simple but symbolic. For anyone who has never loved

and lost a dog it would be meaningless, but for anyone who has loved, lived and lost a friend like Inca, I think it is a rather touching legacy. A growing object of beauty.

For me, that simple ceremony was a way of saying thank you. Thank you to a little black dog who helped shape my life. She changed it in ways I never thought possible. Inca brought me so much happiness and pleasure over the years. We shared so many adventures together. It seemed fitting that one chapter would end here in the park where it all began.

My most prized possession is a painting – a painting of Inca. Marina commissioned the artists Oli and Suzy to paint her. Oli and Suzy are two of the most talented artists of their generation; they have focused on wildlife, painting everything from African wild dogs and elephants to Amazonian anacondas and polar bears. Apart from the fact that the duo paint together, their individuality comes in the interaction of the animal with the work of art – elephant footprints, claws, even shark bites.

Marina somehow persuaded them to paint Inca and had planned to give me the painting for my 40th birthday. It was a sign of just how much Inca meant to me . . . and that Marina knew it. This wasn't any old painting. This was something special.

Marina gave me the painting early. Inca had died a few weeks after its completion and Marina thought it would bring me some comfort.

I cried when I saw it. It is perfect. It IS Inca, made all the more poignant by her muddy paw prints all over it. The slouch. Her paws. Her head tilt.

I love that painting. It makes me smile. As Dr Seuss wrote,

'Don't cry because it is over, Smile because it happened'.

It is the sad inevitability that we will almost always outlast our dogs.

After she died, I wrote her story for the *Sunday Telegraph*. I received hundreds if not thousands of letters and emails. Strangers would stop me on the street. My story was just one of millions and millions of Labrador tales – all slightly different, all with the same hero, the loyal, kind, thoughtful, generous, hungry friend.

Why is it that dogs have such a powerful pull over us all? What is it about our four-legged friends that can reduce a grown man who has rowed the Atlantic and been swimming with wild Nile crocodiles to a weeping wreck?

My father has experienced the power of bereavement for over forty years. Mine was far from unique. Many people are more devastated at the loss of their beloved dog than they are at the loss of a family member. Perhaps it is because the bond is so unique. It is one of utter physical dependence from the dog, like that of a carer and their charge.

In many ways it is more intense than many other relation-ships, both physically and psychologically. The bond between person and dog is very physical – hugging, stroking and in many cases kissing. For many people it might be their only form of physical contact. Even for those who are married, there is argu-ably more physical touch between the human and the dog.

Humans can show their emotions between one another using words or even gestures, but for a dog it is often physical. I wonder whether it is this intimacy that tightens the bond.

The physiological connection is also unique. We are more

likely to be honest to our dogs than to another person. When I say honest, I don't mean that we lie to other people, but we are less likely to 'edit' what we do or say. Mainly this is because the conversation is one way – there is no way the dog will ever repeat what it has heard or even seen.

How many of us have whispered our worries and our woes to our dog? I have unburdened myself of countless worries over the years. Inca was privy to more secrets than any member of my family. I've no doubt this is the reason the dog becomes and extension of you. You can really be yourself with your dog. I mean, 'singing, dancing, and funny voices' yourself.

In a constantly shifting world, a dog can be a stabilising force. For me in particular, Inca provided me with a stabilising consistency in an ever-changing world. She was there to witness the key moments in my life. My loss of anonymity. My struggle to reintegrate into society after my year in isolation. My various relationships. Travel. Work. Fame.

My world is one of nomadic travel. For more than 15 years I have travelled the globe. I spend more than seven months away from home. There is no consistency in my life. Family, of course, has since changed all of that, but through my bachelor years, Inca was the one consistency in an unstructured world.

I would travel off to remote corners of the globe to return to my little Notting Hill flat and Inca was always there to greet me. Of course, it meant she had two families, as it was my parents who always looked after her while I was away. But Inca never held it against me. She never complained. She was always there, wagging her tail and leaning against my leg.

It is a combination of that consistency with unfailing loyalty that leads to this inseparable bond. A dog, you see, will always forgive. A stroke and a handful of food and all is forgotten.

Humans are so much more complex. You can't really argue with a dog.

There is nothing quite like waking to a dog licking your face. A house feels empty without the greeting of a wagging tail. A five-minute trip to the corner shop for some milk is rewarded with a welcome like we've been gone for a year. It makes us feel special.

Dogs simply don't have the emotional complexity, the layers that we have. And at the top of that list, I'd argue, is the Labrador. I would say that, wouldn't I? But as this book has proved, I am far from the first and certainly won't be the last lover of Labradors.

A Labrador offers much more than just loyalty and love; they combine those qualities with a subdued intelligence and an eagerness to please.

Inca was the best thing that ever happened to me, but I'm far from unique in that situation – as these pages have demonstrated, Labradors have achieved a global dominance that is quite extraordinary.

There are, of course, plenty of other popular breeds, many of which share numerous similar personality traits – the Golden Retriever, for example – but the Labrador is still king.

'Will you get another dog?' was the mantra for the couple of years after Inca died. I needed time. I couldn't bear the thought of another dog so soon after. We still had Maggi and it was simply too soon.

But as all Labrador owners will know, their coarse long hairs – be they black, yellow or chocolate – get into your soul.

Labradors get under your skin. And before long you begin to crack as you are haunted by the Labrador spirit, willing you to begin again.

The Labrador has morphed from fisherman's friend into man's best friend over the course of a hundred years. Dependable and biddable, they have evolved into one of the planet's most popular breeds.

Celebrated in popular culture, loved by dictators and presidents, valued by the military and prized by charities, the Labrador has become a jack of all trades. Multitalented and multifaceted, all of these credentials are wrapped up in a dog that also looks perfect.

Their size, shape, head, ears, eyes, nose and tail are all perfectly proportioned. Look at a seal and you will see a Lab. I'd argue that not only have they evolved in their tasks, but also in their appearance. They have become irresistible. I defy the hardest of souls to walk past a Labrador and not feel compelled to stroke it.

I've never really trusted someone who doesn't like a Lab. What isn't there to like?

I still miss Inca. I think of her often. The thought of getting another dog felt so disloyal. Inviting another dog into her home and her car just felt wrong.

But eventually we all relent . . .

CHAPTER THIRTEEN

A PERFECT STORM

All good things come to an end.

It's incredible how something or someone can come into your life and turn it inside out. The arrival of my first child changed my life; the arrival of my second child, my daughter, changed it forever.

But sometimes life throws you a curve ball. It catches you off guard. My third child was stillborn. I don't want to dwell. It was the worst time of my life, from which my wife and I will never really recover. You learn to deal with it, but it's always there. During that long week in an Austrian hospital we tried to focus on what we had rather than what we'd lost. We buried Willem and tried to console ourselves with dreams about our future.

'We're getting a puppy,' smiled Marina. A tear trickled down my cheek.

Neither of us was under any illusion that a puppy would ever make up for such a traumatic, life-changing loss, but it would be something to look forward to, a break from the bleak storm in which we found ourselves trapped.

A puppy would give us something positive to focus on as a family.

There was never any question in my mind as to what it would be. We'd get a Labrador puppy.

The children were delirious with excitement; since the day he could talk, Ludo had resolved to follow my father, his grandpa, into veterinary medicine. He cares and worries about animals more than any other child I've ever met. His teachers invariably comment on this compassionate streak.

I suppose it shouldn't be that surprising given that it was dogs that brought both his parents and his grandparents together.

I called up Sussie Wiles, the breeder from whom Henry Holland Hibbert had got his Labradors, the closest I had come to the original progenitors.

'A litter has just been born,' she said.

'There are four black bitches and you can have first choice.'

It was surely destiny.

On the day that we were to meet our puppy, I woke up at 5am. My heart was racing. I hadn't had this kind of feeling since I was a child on Christmas Eve. The anticipation and excitement of the stocking. I sipped a coffee alone downstairs. It is a rare moment of silence in our house before the children stir.

I felt a mixture of excited nervousness. In just a few hours' time everything would change forever.

The careful dynamic of our household would change. It had taken several years of nappies and sleepless nights to reach this place and now we were going to shift it again.

My pensive reflections were soon interrupted by a cacophony of children. Breakfast, dressing, teeth, old dog walking and soon we were in the car heading west.

It's funny how sometimes you spend your life searching for something, only to find it right underneath your nose. And it seemed to be in the most unlikely of places: Uxbridge.

My life has taken me to the furthest corners of the world and to each and every corner of the United Kingdom, and now we were on our way to Uxbridge in west London, barely twenty minutes from where we lived. I had passed the sign many times. I must admit I had only been to Uxbridge once before in my life, nearly 12 years ago, when for some inexplicable reason I was sent there by Graham Norton to do a live insert from the town centre into his Saturday night TV show. If I remember correctly, I was standing in a temporary DJ booth in the middle of the city centre being pelted by rubbish from drunken local youth. Happy days.

Of course, this wasn't our first trip to Uxbridge. We had made several visits from the first time we had met the litter. Marina hadn't been so sure about getting a puppy from a breeder; she was wary about it, being more keen to rehome or adopt a dog from an animal shelter. She had experienced first hand the health issues that had dogged the pure-bred Inca's life and she was naturally concerned that we would merely repeat the process with another Labrador. But it's incredible the sway that a litter of pups can have on attitudes and moods. I genuinely believe that if we catapulted a litter of pups into almost any situation, they could diffuse the tension. Conflict, fights, arguments could all be settled with a cuddle from a newborn pup.

I could see Marina melt as she cuddled each and every puppy in the litter. Ludo and Iona, too, had fallen silent as they hugged, squeezed and nuzzled the black and yellow fur.

We had agreed that we would take a black bitch. (I hate those two words; they make you feel like a racist bigot. In one of the strangest email correspondences I have ever had, I found myself in the very unlikely and rather worrying position of asking Prince William if he knew of any black bitches at Sandringham.) Labrador colour is a personal and probably quite an emotive issue. In some ways, a little like the breed, I think people often choose the same colour with every dog they get.

I grew up with blonde Golden Retrievers. My childhood was dominated by their blonde hair that coated my clothes in yellow and white swathes, but long before I chose Inca, I had always known I wanted a black Labrador. I can't say why. I just wanted one.

Many of the dog owners I met during my Labrador research had insisted that black was the only true authentic colour, and that yellow and brown had come latterly. Black, after all, was arguably the best camouflage for those out hunting or shooting, their colour merging with the environment.

Of course, by choosing a black Labrador, as I had with Inca, I had merely replaced the swathes of wispy thin blonde Golden Retriever hair that had dominated my childhood, with the brittle black hairs of the Labrador. Inca's hair had plagued me for more than a decade. I used to dread her moults. They happened like clockwork. Hair would cascade from her body like a waterfall, forming tides of fur around the house. She would leave perfect impressions of her body on the bed, carpet and rug. Like the police chalks of murder victims drawn at the scene of a crime, Inca would leave silhouettes of herself. You could always tell exactly where she had been.

I would try to remove as much fur as I could by hand to minimise the fur tsunami around the house. I would stand over her and, using my fingers like a giant comb, I would drag at her fur. Armfuls of the stuff would fall to the ground; puffed with air, I would create mini mountains of the stuff. I filled whole bin bags and still the fur fell.

It's one of the downsides of having a dog that moults, particularly if they have a big thick lion's mane of a coat like Inca, but these are some of the sacrifices we make as owners.

As for sex, I have only ever known girl dogs, or bitches to give them their correct terminology. Why 'bitch' I have no idea. I always think it makes me sound like Tupac Shakur or some gang member from the Bronx.

Like the choice of breed and colour, sex is a very instinctive choice. Perhaps if you have never had a dog before, you might find yourself more easily swayed, but I have only ever had female dogs. Over the years I have built up a general stereotype of male dogs. They are brutish and arrogant. They race up with their head held high in an authoritative manner. Most fights I have ever witnessed have invariably involved male dogs. They are much more physical than bitches (there's that word again), using their bodies to assert their authority.

How many times have I had to shake a male dog from my leg after it has mistaken it for a female dog? I reckon we have all experienced a humping dog on our leg, but I reckon I've had it more than most. Maybe it is the symptom of being a vet's son, or perhaps I just have a really fit leg, but I have lost count of the times I've had to shake a humping dog from my leg. I'm not sure who it's more embarrassing for either. The dog, the owner or the humpee?

And if it's not humping, it's leg cocking. Where female dogs always seem rather elegant with their urination, squatting unobtrusively, their male counterparts seem to relish the opportunity to cock their legs little and often . . . on anything and everything.

Just a few months ago I was walking in the park when a large Weimaraner ran up to me and confidently lifted its leg against me, releasing a cascade of pee down my leg before I even had time to react, before racing off. Leg cocking is used to mark territory and it is this territorial character that I have always found a little overbearing in the male.

That is not to say, incidentally, that bitches are perfect. On the contrary, there are plenty of aspects that are just as difficult, if not worse, the hardest being the season. Why it's called a season rather than a period like in women I have no idea. I have always assumed it is something to do with their breeding season. Unfortunately there is no such thing as a dog tampon. If you have never had a female dog then I'll leave the mess to your imagination.

When I first met Marina, she used to dress her dog Maggi in special doggy 'pants' complete with a hole for the tail. Poor Maggi would skulk around looking humiliated. They were, of course, only meant to be worn around the house and in the car, but she would often end of walking from one to the other in her pants. If dogs could blush she would have been puce.

So here we were, making a decision about a new dog. We

handled each and every pup, examining their legs, tails, heads. To be honest, they were barely two weeks old. Their eyes were yet to open and the only distinguishing factor was their colour. We had a selection of six black pups, four of which were bitches. Of these four, apart from a tiny variable in size, there was nothing in it.

Pat White had told me of the 'puppy aptitude' test, a way of scientifically choosing the correct puppy for you. 'Biddability and compatibility,' she had explained, 'are the key traits in the correct dog.'

'Whatever you do, don't let the children choose the puppy,' she had warned.

'So which one do you want?' Marina had asked Ludo and Iona as we cuddled the litter.

Despite the best advice, I think both Marina and I are driven by instinct. We both knew deep down that it would be nearly impossible to choose a puppy using any sort of scientific reason at two weeks.

As it happened, Sheila instructed us to return a month later, at six weeks, once the puppies had developed more of their characters and personalities.

Since that first visit we had returned several times to watch the growing pups. On the penultimate visit we had been asked to make our decision.

Even at six weeks, there was very little to differentiate them. Some were a little more sleepy and docile, but that was probably because they were a little sleepy. As I have already explained, I am often guided by instinct. To be honest. I am a firm believer in destiny. What will be will be.

It came down to two pups, only distinguishable from one

another by their slight size, variation. I had chosen a slightly larger one than Marina and the children. Instinctively I think I had wanted a Labrador on the larger size, while Marina wanted a more 'portable' version that could be easily squeezed into the car between bags and children.

'Paper, Rock, Scissors,' smiled Marina. 'Best of three wins.'

Marina and the children won. Of course they won. They chose the small pup with a pretty face. A thin piece of pink wool was tied around her neck. She would be ours and we hers. That little pink necklace marked out our future together.

It had felt strange leaving her for another two weeks, knowing that she was our pup. But now we were returning to bring her home. To envelop her into the Fogle Family fold.

We pulled up at the farmhouse.

I can remember collecting Inca like it was yesterday. By coincidence it was less than thirty minutes from here. So much had happened in the fifteen years since I had picked up Inca. My life had changed beyond recognition. I had been a young, single, naive 25-year-old still living with Mum and Dad when I had collected Inca. Now I was here with my own family.

I can even remember picking up my childhood dogs, Liberty and Lexington. There is something so monumental about the day you collect a dog. It's not on the scale of the birth of a child, but there is nonetheless something monumental and life-changing about it. It is a moment when two, or in this case five, lives collide.

We knocked on the door. Sussie answered and we went through to the front room where all the pups were still in the whelping box. The pups were now eight weeks old and a riot of dogs raced towards us.

There at the front was the little pink-collared pup. We scooped her up and cradled her.

There is something a little sad about taking a pup from the warmth, safety and comfort of its brothers and sisters. For eight weeks they had eaten, slept and played together. She had long been weened from her mother but this was still a moment when she would be taken from her nest.

I suppose it's all about perspective. The little pup may be leaving its siblings but it is also heading for a loving home.

I love this idea that throughout the world these litters of Labradors have been primed and prepared by their mothers to bring love and companionship. I am a sucker for anthropomorphism. I can't help but imagine the pups being tutored in how to be as cute and kind as possible.

David Attenborough once hypothesised that dogs are arguably the most conniving parasite on Earth, who through evolution have become as sweet and loving as possible in order to ingratiate themselves into our homes.

Is there anyone in the world who doesn't like a puppy? Kittens, calves, lambs . . . they all have a cuteness, but none of them really comes close to a puppy, with their perfect little faces. A puppy has the ability to melt the facade of the toughest gangster or the hardest politician.

The 'parasite' hypothesis goes on to speculate that through cuteness, puppies have evolved to get closer and closer to man. First by living within communities, then into gardens, next houses, and now, for many of us, even our beds.

Our beds? If you aren't a dog lover, look away now, though I doubt you would have chosen this book in the first place unless you had already been hypnotised by the allure of the dog. What is it that encourages us to allow these animals onto, and in many cases into, our beds? They are the descendants of wild animals, after all.

But that is the whole point. The puppy has evolved to look as sweet and cute as possible in order to secure its place with mankind. Now the same could be said for any puppy, but I disagree. I think the Labrador puppy has a particular, indefinable allure. Just look at the popularity of the Labrador puppy in marketing. They are everywhere. Hollywood films choose them as the ultimate family pet and everything from loo roll to beer has used them in advertising.

Sussie handed me a little bag that contained the puppy's worldly possessions – a worn toy pheasant and a small blanket from the box. Both would bring the smell of familiarity to help her adapt to her new life.

Clutching her tightly, we walked to the car. Marina held her on her lap as we waved goodbye.

It was a journey to a new life for us all.

For Marina and me, it was a new chapter in our marriage together. Dogs had brought us together, but the dogs had always had personal familiarity. The puppy years of both Maggi and my late dog Inca remained a mystery to one another. I had never known Maggi as a pup. I had seen the photographs and heard the tales, but for me she was Maggi, the older dog.

Now we were embarking on a new adventure with a puppy together, *en famille*.

We weren't really sure how Maggi would react. There is no kind way to introduce a puppy to a geriatric dog. I worried about how Maggi would interpret the situation. 'Here we go', she says, 'they think I'm about to kick the bucket, so here's a little pup to replace me.'

It is impossible to explain a situation to a dog. Excuses or explanations don't cut it.

Still clutching the puppy under my arm, we walked into the house. Maggi was fast asleep on the sofa. Since she had turned 14, she had taken to sleeping for most of the day in a happy, contented slumber. The commotion and noise of squealing children woke her and I could see her sniffing the air.

We placed the little pup on the floor and Maggi sniffed her briefly before wandering off. I wish I knew what she was thinking. The puppy was deliriously happy to meet another dog.

We still hadn't named her. Naming a dog is not like naming a child. There is no need to discuss and speculate how the child is going to feel in years to come. No need to second-guess the teasing opportunities that come with a name. A dog's name is much more flexible.

It was a choice between Tatty and Storm. Why? You may well ask. I wish I could come up with a fantastic anecdote or yarn, but the simple truth is that I liked both names. I had very nearly called Inca Tatty, and I had always liked Storm or Stormy.

We got the children to call out the name at the top of their lungs to see which one tripped off the tongue more easily, and Storm won.

Storm she was.

From the minute she arrived into our home, this little pup became a firm part of the family. It's amazing the power of a pup to bond a family. Even Maggi lowered her guard and began to enjoy this little bundle of fur's company.

Ever since my little boy, Ludo, was born, he has wanted to work with animals. Ludo loves animals. I mean really loves them. Last summer, in Austria, we were cooking ribs on the barbecue. They were delicious but we simply couldn't get Ludo to try them. Normally an adventurous eater, he kept refusing. Eventually, after a huge amount of bribery, I managed to persuade him to try a little. He nibbled a sparrow's peck from one of the ribs and told me triumphantly he didn't like them. Now I'd believe him if this was liver or pâté or sushi, but these were the tastiest ribs I'd ever tried. It was as if he didn't want to like them.

A few days later we were in the car, when, apropos of nothing, Ludo suddenly piped up, 'Daddy,' he said, while peering through the window, 'do you know why I didn't like the ribs?' He continued, 'It was because I didn't like the thought,' he explained. 'I didn't like the thought of eating from the little animal's ribs.'

I was blown away. This was coming from a five-year-old boy. My own son. He decided on his own valuation to question eating various forms of meat. He had already told us that he didn't like beef, but now he was explaining that it was the thought, not the taste, that he didn't like.

'Why do we have to kill animals?' he asked.

For the first time I was genuinely lost for a satisfactory answer. I could have said it's because we are omnivores and that we need to eat meat, but he had a valid question. My own son was challenging my own decisions and sentiments. Suddenly I didn't really have an answer. Why would we welcome dogs into our homes while at the same time happily allow people to kill animals on our behalf to sate our appetite? It seems so contradictory. How can you love one animal enough to allow it into your house while you happily eat another?

I have often worried that society has lost any sense of connection between the meat we buy in a supermarket, or even from a butcher, and the living animal from which it comes. We live in a sanitised society where the horrors of the abattoir are hidden behind doors. Meat is packaged to look less like meat. It's as if we don't want to admit to ourselves the provenance of the bacon or the burger. It has become an abstract food, not much different to a chocolate bar or an apple.

Allowing a dog into your home provokes more thoughtful debate. Ludo's deep love of animals, and in particular Maggi and now Storm, has led him to question our animal morals.

Storm is our dog, but deep down she is really Ludo's. Ludo loves that little dog more than anything else. It takes me back to my own childhood and the deep love I had for my two dogs when I was growing up. Ludo would scoop little Storm up under her belly and march her around the house. He would place her into her bed, and from the beginning he would help to feed her and come with me to the park to walk her. A puppy brings responsibility, which is an important and joyful lesson for children.

This little pup has re-energised our home. With her youthful enthusiasm she has created a new dynamic. In the morning she sits next to the bed and stares. Even with my eyes closed I can feel those Labrador eyes like laser beams, willing me to wake from my slumber. At the first sign of movement, she comes closer and lifts her front legs onto the bed and licks my face.

The excitement with which she greets each morning is infectious. She wakes long before the children. I scoop her up and take her down to the garden. Just me and her. It reminds me of the time when Inca was my sole companion, all those years ago. We'd wander down to the barn together, light the wood-burning stove and sit there alone. Just the two of us.

Fifteen years later and I was doing the same with Storm. The slouch, the head tilt, the protruding back leg. The echoes of Inca are uncanny.

The Labrador must be one of the most versatile breeds in the world. Guide dogs, hearing dogs, police dogs, bomb detection dogs, drug sniffer dogs, war dogs, search-and-rescue dogs, truffle-sniffing dogs, cancer-sniffing dogs, epilepsy dogs, autism dogs, assistance dogs, fishermen's dogs, politicans' dogs, rock 'n' roll dogs, family dogs . . . the list goes on.

I know it sounds saccharine, but these loyal black dogs have been my guardian angels over the years, silently guiding and directing me. They are always there. Loyal, kind, happy and optimistic. As we have discovered, they have extraordinary versatility as well as an untarnished and unwavering loyalty. They offer a tonic to many of the ills of the world. We can learn a great deal from the Labrador.

The humble Labrador has changed my life. It is little surprise then that the Labrador has become the world's most popular breed. Man's Best Best Friend . . . Forever.

INDEX

ACKNOWLEDGEMENTS

Thanks . . .

To Sarah Edworthy who helped me gather the history and unpick the story of the Labrador.

To my father for introducing me to my lifelong passion for dogs.

To Sussie Wiles and family for our beautiful little Storm and to Richard Edwards for his useful comments on the manuscript.

To Sam McColl for loving our dogs even more than we do.

To Myles Archibald for hanging on so long and to the team at HarperCollins.

To Julian Alexander and the team at LAW.

To everyone who helped me while writing this book.